MW01011970

The Light Before Christmas

HILDA BUTLER FARR

The light before Christmas is something divine
Which glows like a star in the sky,
And people are lifted above dull routine
As each day of December rolls by.

It shines in the faces of young and of old
As they meet in a crowded store.
The same story prevails on every street,
Affecting the rich and the poor.

It beams and it glistens with promises new,
Reminding us all once again
Of the babe in a manger in Bethlehem
Who became the Saviour of men.

It shimmers in every candle's bright flame,
In windows where trees are ablaze.
There's radiance in the atmosphere
As we listen to carols of praise.

So people are lifted above dull routine
As each day of December rolls by.
The light before Christmas is something divine
Which glows like a star in the sky.

"A diamond shines no brighter than that lovely Christmas star."

JANE K. NUTT

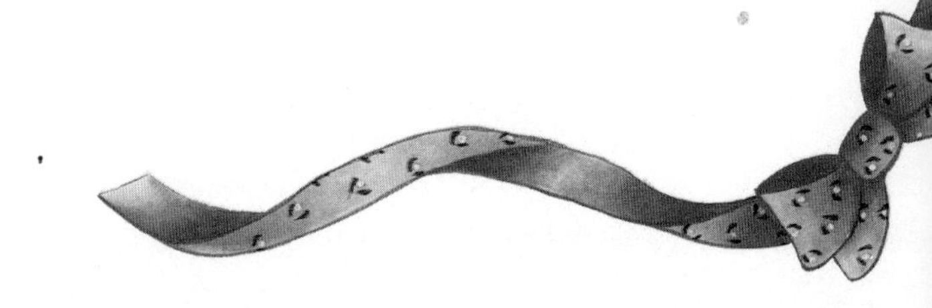

SUGAR

A Christmas Wish

EUGENE FIELD

I'd like a stocking made for a giant
And a meeting house full of toys;
Then I'd go out in a happy hunt
For the poor little girls and boys.
Up the street and down the street,
And across and over the town,
I'd search and find them every one,
Before the sun went down.

One would want a new jackknife
Sharp enough to cut;
One would long for a doll with hair,
And eyes that open and shut;
One would ask for a china set
With dishes all to her mind;
One would wish a Noah's ark
With beasts of every kind.

Some would like a doll's cook stove
And a little toy washtub;
Some would prefer a little drum
For a noisy rub-a-dub;
Some would wish for a story book,
And some for a set of blocks;
Some would be wild with happiness
Over a new toolbox.

And some would rather have little shoes
And other things warm to wear;
For many children are very poor,
And the winter is hard to bear;
I'd buy soft flannels for little frocks,
And a thousand stockings or so,
And the jolliest little coats and cloaks
To keep out the frost and snow.

I'd load a wagon with caramels
And candy of every kind,
And buy all the almond and pecan nuts
And taffy that I could find;
And barrels and barrels of oranges
I'd scatter right in the way,
So the children would find them the very first thing
When they awake on Christmas day.

"Along about Christmas there's laughter and cheer
That keep it the happiest time of the year."

LILLIE D. CHAFFIN

Scents of Holiday Home

TASTES THAT EVOKE MEMORIES OF CHRISTMASES PAST

Christmas Eve Clam Chowder

At our house, Mother always served clam chowder on Christmas Eve. She made it the day before and let it "ripen" in the refrigerator. Hot and rich, the combination of hearty potato pieces and delicate, tender clam bits filled our bodies in preparation for Christmas Eve church services that enriched our souls.—Lucy Riley

On December 23, drain 1 pint shucked clams, chopped, or two 6½-ounce cans minced clams, reserving liquid. Set clams aside. Add enough water to reserved liquid to measure 2 cups liquid; set aside. In a large saucepan, fry 2 slices chopped bacon until crisp; remove bits of bacon and set aside. Add reserved liquid; 4 medium potatoes, peeled and diced; and ½ cup chopped onion to the saucepan. Cook, covered, about 15 minutes or until potatoes are tender. Stir in clams, 2 cups milk, and 1 cup light cream. In a small bowl, combine ½ cup milk and 3 tablespoons all-purpose flour. Add flour mixture to chowder. Cook and stir until bubbly. Cook 1 minute more. Add ½ teaspoon Worcestershire sauce, ¾ teaspoon salt, and dash pepper. Sprinkle bacon pieces on top. Serve with freshly baked bread. Makes 6 servings.

Moravian Sand Tarts

These cookies are patterned after the traditional cookies of the Moravians of Bethlehem, Pennsylvania, and Mom and I began baking them for holiday gifts when I was old enough to help only by licking the bowl. The cinnamon scents of these cookies baking always transport me back home to my mother's kitchen of forty years ago.—Glenda Marche

In a large bowl, cream 1 cup unsalted butter with 1 teaspoon vanilla extract, ½ teaspoon salt, and 1¼ cups confectioners' sugar until fluffy, about 3 minutes. Add 3 eggs, one at a time, beating well after each addition. Add ½ teaspoon baking soda and 2 cups all-purpose flour, stirring well to mix. Chill dough overnight.

Remove dough from refrigerator to soften about 30 minutes before rolling out. Preheat oven to 350° F. In a small bowl, combine ¼ cup granulated sugar and 1 teaspoon ground cinnamon; set aside. Roll out half the dough on a floured surface to about ⅛ inch thick. Cut out cookies with a 2-inch cutter.

Transfer to a lightly greased baking sheet. Brush the cookies with beaten egg white, then sprinkle on the sugar-cinnamon mixture. Press a pecan half into the center of each cookie. Bake in the upper third of the oven 7 to 10 minutes. (The cookies will bake faster on dark pans.) Remove to a rack to cool. Makes about 6 dozen cookies.

Steaming Spiced Cider

At our home, we always set aside one evening just before Christmas for caroling with our church choir. And we always ended the evening at my folks' home for bowls of hot buttery popcorn and steaming spiced apple cider. After several hours of tramping around in the snow and cold of a Milwaukee December evening, the familiar scent of the cider began invading my senses even before we were finished caroling, and the memory of the tart yet sweet taste from that cup has yet to be equaled for me.—Lennie Garfield

In a large pot, combine 2 quarts apple cider, 3 cinnamon sticks, 40 whole cloves, and 1 teaspoon ground nutmeg; bring to a boil. Simmer for 15 minutes. Stir in 2 cups freshly squeezed orange juice, ½ cup fresh lemon juice, and 2 strips orange peel. Serve hot with a whole cinnamon stick. Makes 9 quarts.

Christmas Morning Orange Muffins

At our house, we kids used to get up at three o'clock in the morning and sneak into the living room to see what Santa had left us. The house was cold at that time of the morning; but our shivers were from excitement as well as the chill. By eight o'clock, however, Mom and Dad were up, the fireplace had been stoked, and the smell of orange muffins was wafting from the kitchen. For me, warmth, family, love, and Christmas remain wrapped up in the scent of Christmas morning orange muffins.—Mae Henry

Preheat oven to 400° F. Lightly grease 12 muffin cups or line with paper liners. In a large bowl, combine 2 cups all-purpose flour, ½ cup granulated sugar, 2½ teaspoons baking powder, and ¼ teaspoon salt. In a smaller bowl, combine ½ cup orange juice, 2 tablespoons milk, ⅓ cup melted and cooled butter, 1 lightly beaten large egg, 1 teaspoon vanilla, and ¼ teaspoon baking soda. Whisk until blended. Stir the wet ingredients into the dry and combine with as few strokes as possible. Stir in 3 teaspoons grated orange peel and ½ cup chopped pecans. Spoon batter into prepared muffin cups, filling each about two-thirds full. Bake 15 to 20 minutes, or until golden.

Meanwhile, in a small saucepan, combine 2 teaspoons grated orange peel, ⅓ cup fresh orange juice, and ⅓ cup granulated sugar. Bring to a boil, stirring to dissolve sugar. Turn heat down and let simmer until slightly thickened, about 4 to 5 minutes. Let cool slightly. The glaze should be thin enough to soak into the muffins. After bringing the muffins out of the oven, let cool 2 to 3 minutes. Brush the tops with the warm glaze, or drizzle over the tops with a spoon. Serve warm. Makes 12 muffins.

As Ye Sow . . .

DOROTHY CANFIELD FISHER

Casually, not that she was especially interested, just to say something, she asked as she handed out the four o'clock pieces of bread and peanut butter, "Well, what Christmas songs are you learning in your room this year?"

There was a moment's pause. Then the three little boys, her own and the usual two of his playmates, told her soberly, first one speaking, then another, "We're not going to be let to sing. Teacher don't want us in the Christmas entertainment." Their round, eight-year-old faces were grave.

"Well!" said the mother. "For goodness' sakes, why not?"

Looking down at his feet, her own small David answered sadly, "Teacher says we can't sing good enough."

"Well enough," corrected his mother mechanically.

"Well enough," he repeated as mechanically.

One of the others said in a low tone, "She says we can't carry a tune. She's only going to let kids sing in the entertainment that can carry a tune. . . ."

Inwardly the mother broke into a mother's rage at a teacher. "So that's what she says, does she? What's she for, anyhow, if not to teach children what they don't know. The idea! As if she'd say she would teach arithmetic only to those who are good at it already." . . .

She drew in a deep breath and put the loaf of bread away. Then she said quietly, "Well, lots of kids your age can't carry a tune. Not till they've learned. How'd you like to practice your song with me? I could play the air on the piano afternoons, after school. You'd get the hang of it that way."

They brightened, they bit off great chunks of their snacks, and said, thickly, that that would be swell. They did not say they would be grateful to her, or regretted being a bother to her, busy as she always was. She did not expect them to. In fact it would have startled her if they had. She was the mother of four.

So while the after-school bread-and-butter was being eaten, washed down with gulps of milk, while the November-muddy rubbers were taken off, the mother pushed to the back of the stove the interrupted rice pudding, washed her hands at the sink, looked into the dining room where her youngest, Janey, was waking her dolls up from naps taken in the dining-room chairs, and took off her apron. Together the four went into the living room to the piano.

"What song is it your room is to sing?"

"It came upon the midnight," said the three little boys, speaking at once.

"That's a nice one," she commented, reaching for the battered songbook on top of the piano. "This is the way it goes." She played the air and sang the first two lines. "That'll be enough to start on," she told them. "Now," she gave them the signal to start.

They started. She had given them food for body and heart. Refreshed, heartened, with unquestioning confidence in a grownup's ability to achieve whatever she planned, they opened their mouths happily and sang out.

"It came upon the midnight clear
That glorious song of old. . . ."

At the end of that phrase she stopped abruptly and for an instant bowed her head over the keys. Her feeling about Teacher made a right-about turn. There was a pause.

But she was a mother, not a teacher. She lifted her head, turned a smiling face on the three bellowing children. "I tell you what," she said. "The way, really, to learn a tune is just one note after another. The reason why a teacher can't get everybody in her room up to singing in tune is because she'd have to teach each person separately—unless they happen to be naturally good at singing. That would take too much time, you see. A teacher has such a lot of children to see to. . . .

"Listen," said the mother, "I'll strike just the two first notes on the piano: 'It came.'" She struck the notes, she sang them clearly. Full of good will, the little boys sang with her. She stopped. Breathed hard.

"Not quite," she said, with a false smile, "pret-t-ty good. Close to it. But not quite, yet. I think we'd better take it one note at a time. Bill, you try it." . . .

Without hesitation, Bill sang "I-i-it" loudly. After he had, the mother, as if fascinated, kept her eyes fixed on his still open mouth. Finally, "Try again," she said. "But first, listen. Oracularly she told them, "Half of carrying a tune is listening first."

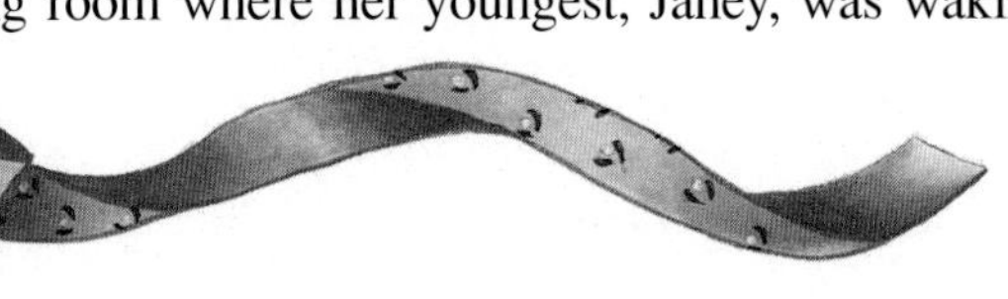

She played the note again. And again. And again. Then, rather faintly, she said, "Peter, you sing it now."

At the note emitted by Peter, she let out her breath, as if she had been under water and just come up. "Fine!" she said. "Now we're getting somewhere! David, your urn." David was her own. "Just that one note. No, not quite. A little higher. Not quite so high." She was in a panic. What could she do? "Wait," she told David. "Try ust breathing it out, not loud at all. Maybe you can get it better."...

That evening when she told her husband about it, after the children had gone to bed, she ended her story with a vehement "You never heard anything like it in your life, Harry. Never. It was appalling! You can't imagine what it was!"

"Oh, yes I can too," he said over his temporarily owered newspaper. "I've heard plenty of tone-deaf kids ollering. I know what they sound like. There are people, ou know, who really can't carry a tune. You probably never could teach them. Why don't you give it up?"...

That was reasonable, after all, thought the mother. Yes, that was the sensible thing to do. She would be sensible, for once, and give it up. With everything she had o do, she would just be reasonable and sensible about his.

So the next morning, when she was downtown oing her marketing, she turned in at the public library nd asked for books about teaching music to children. Rather young children, about eight years old, she xplained.

The librarian, enchanted with someone who did not sk for a light, easy-reading novel, brought her two ooks, which she took away with her....

Assiduous reading of those two reference books on eaching music taught her that there were other approaches than a frontal attack on the tune they wanted o sing. She tried out ear-experiments with them, of which she would never have dreamed without her library books. She discovered to her dismay that sure enough, just as the authors of the books said, the little boys were musically so far below scratch that, without seeing which piano keys she struck, they had no idea whether a note was higher or lower than the one before . She adapted and invented musical "games" to train heir ear for this. The boys standing in a row, their backs o the piano, listening to hear whether the second note was "up hill or down hill" from the first note, thought it s good a game as any other, rather funnier than most because so new to them. They laughed raucously over each other's mistakes, kidded and joshed each other, ran a contest to see who came out best, while the mother, aproned for cooking, her eye on the clock, got up and down for hurried forays into the kitchen where she was trying to get supper....

She faltered. Many times. She saw the ironing heaped high, or Janey was in bed with a cold, and as four o'clock drew near, she said to herself, "Now today I'll just tell the boys that I cannot go on with this. We're not getting anywhere, anyhow."

So when they came storming in, hungry and cheerful and full of unquestioning certainty that she would not close that door she had half-opened for them, she laid everything aside and went to the piano.

As a matter of fact, they were getting somewhere. She had bean so beaten down that she was genuinely surprised at the success of the exercises ingeniously devised by the authors of those books. Even with their backs to the piano, the boys could now tell, infallibly, whether a second note was above or below the first one. Sure. They even thought it distinctly queer that they had not been able to, at first. "Never paid any attention to it, before," was their own accurate surmise as to the reason.

They paid attention now, their interest aroused by their first success, by the incessant practicing of the others in their classroom, by the Christmas-entertainment thrill which filled the schoolhouse with suspense. Although they were allowed no part in it, they also paid close attention to the drill given the others. . . . They fully expected—wasn't a grownup teaching them?—to climb those steps to the platform with the others, come the evening of the entertainment....

Just in time, along about the second week of December, they did begin to get somewhere. They could all sound—if they remembered to sing softly and to "listen to themselves"—a note, any note, within their range, she struck on the piano. Little Peter turned out, to his surprise and hers, to have a sweet, clear soprano. The others were—well, all right, good enough.

They started again, very cautiously, to sing that tune, to begin with "It ca-ame," having drawn a deep breath and letting it out carefully. It was right. They were singing true....

After that it went fast; the practicing of the air, their repeating it for the first skeptical, and then thoroughly astonished teacher, their triumphant report at home.

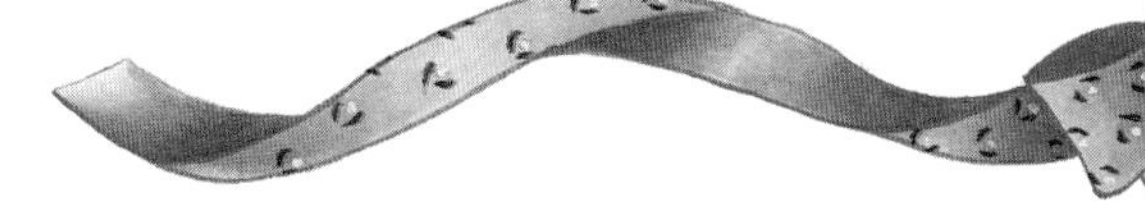

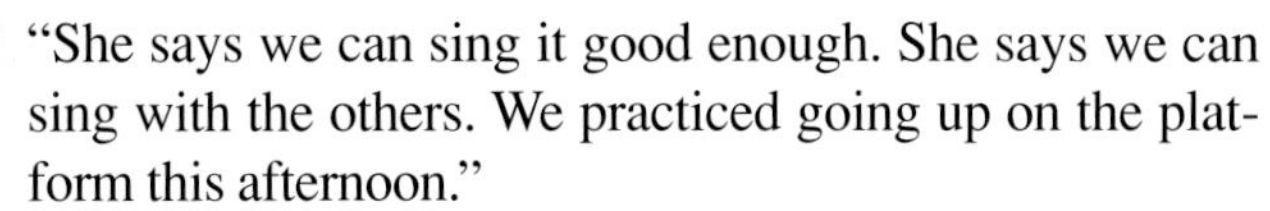

"She says we can sing it good enough. She says we can sing with the others. We practiced going up on the platform this afternoon."

Then the Christmas entertainment. The tramping of class after class up the aisle to the moment of foot-lighted glory; the big eighth-graders' Christmas pantomime, the first graders' wavering performance of a Christmas dance as fairies—or were they snowflakes? . . .

Then it was the turn of the third grade, the eight- and nine-year-olds, the boys clumping up the aisle, the girls switching their short skirts proudly. The careful tiptoeing up the steps to the platform, remembering not to knock their toes on the stair-treads, the two lines of round faces facing the audience, bland and blank in their ignorance of—oh, of everything, thought David's mother, her hand clutching her handbag tensely.

The crash from the piano giving them the tone, all the mouths open,

"It came upo-on the midnight clear
That glorious song of old."

The thin pregnant woman sitting in front of the mother leaned to the shabbily dressed man next to her, with a long breath of relief. "They do real good, don't they?" she whispered proudly.

They did do real good. Teacher's long drill and hers had been successful. It was not howling, it was singing. It had cost the heart's blood, thought the mother, of two women, but it was singing. It would never again be howling, not from those children.

It was even singing with expression—some. There were swelling crescendos, and at the lines

"The world in solemn stillness lay
To hear the angels sing"

The child-voices were hushed in a diminuendo. Part of the mother's very life had been spent in securing her part of that diminuendo. She ached at the thought of the effort that had gone into teaching that hushed tone, of the patience and self-control and endlessly repeated persistence in molding into something shapely the boys' puppy-like inability to think of anything but aimless play. . . .

This had been one of the things that must be done. And she had done it. There he stood, her little David, a fully accredited part of his corner of society, as good as anybody, the threat of the inferiority-feeling averted for this time, ready to face the future with enough self-confidence to cope with what would come next. The door had been slammed in his face. She had pushed it open and he had gone through. . . .

The third grade filed down the steps from the platform and began to march back along the aisle. For a moment, the mother forgot that she was no longer a girl who expected recognition when she had done something creditable. David's class clumped down the aisle. Surely, she thought, David would turn his head to where she sat and thank her with a look. Just this once.

He did turn his head as he filed by. He looked full at his family, at his father, his mother, his kid sister, his big brother and sister from the high school. He gave them a formal, small nod to show that he knew they were there, to acknowledge publicly that they were his family. He even smiled, a very little, stiffly, fleetingly. But his look was not for her. It was just as much for those of his family who had been bored and impatient spectators of her struggle to help him, as for her who had given part of her life to roll that stone uphill, a part of her life she never could get back.

She shifted Janey's weight a little on her knees. Of course. Did mothers ever expect to be thanked? They were to accept what they received, without bitterness, without resentment. After all, that was what mothers worked for—not for thanks, but to do their job. . . .

After all, she thought, hearing vaguely the seventh graders now on the platform (none of her four was in the seventh grade), David was only eight. At that age they were, in personality, completely cocoons, as in their babyhood they had been physical cocoons. The time had not come yet for the inner spirit to stir, to waken, to give a sign that it lived.

It certainly did not stir in young David that winter. There was no sign that it lived. The snowy weeks came and went. He rose, ravenously hungry, ate an enormous breakfast with the family, and clumped off to school with his own third-graders. The usual three stormed back after school, flinging around a cloud of overshoes, caps, mittens, windbreakers. . . . They giggled, laughed raucously, kidded and joshed each other, pushed each other around. . . .

At that age, thought the mother, their souls, if any, were certainly no more than seeds, deep inside their hard, muscular, little-boy flesh. How do souls develop, she wondered occasionally, as she washed dishes, made beds, selected carrots at the market, answered the telephone. How do souls develop out of those rough-and-ready little males? If they do develop? . . .

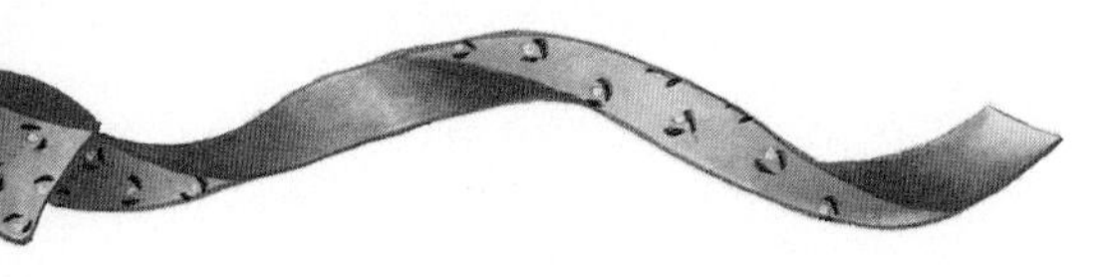

One evening this question tried to push itself into her nind, but was swept aside by her suddenly knowing, as lefinitely as if she had heard a clock strike, or the doorbell ing, that the time had passed for David's return from his evening play-hour with Peter. She looked at her watch. But she did not need to. A sixth sense told her heart, as vith a blow, that he should before this have come pelting home down the hill, plowing the deep snow aside in clouds, hurling himself against the kitchen door. He was late. . . . He must have left the other house some time ago. Peter's mother always sent him home promptly.

She laid down the stocking she was darning, stepped into the dark kitchen, and put her face close to the window to look out. It was a cloudless, cold night. Every detail of the back-yard world was visible, almost transparent, in the pale radiance that fell from the stars. . . .

Then she saw David. He was standing half way down, as still as the frozen night around him. But David never stood still. Knee-deep in the snow he stood, looking all around him. She saw him slowly turn his head to one side, to the other. He lifted his face towards the sky. It was almost frightening to see David stand so still. What could he be looking at? What was there he could be seeing? Or hearing? For as she watched him, the notion crossed her mind that he seemed to be listening. But there was nothing to hear. Nothing.

She did not know what was happening to her little son. Nor what to do. So she did nothing. She stood as still as he, her face at the window, lost in wonder. She saw him finally stir and start slowly, slowly down the path. But David never moved slowly. Had he perhaps had a quarrel with Peter? Had Peter's mother been unkind to him?

It could do no harm now to go to meet him, she thought, and by that time, she could not, anxious as she was, not go to meet him. She opened the kitchen door and stepped out into the dark, under the stars.

He saw her, he came quickly to her, he put his arms around her waist. With every fiber of her body which had borne his, she felt a difference in him. She did not know what to say, so she said nothing.

It was her son who spoke. "It's so still," he said quietly in a hushed voice, a voice she had never heard before. "It's so still!"

He pressed his cheek against her breast. . . . All those stars," he murmured dreamily, "they shine so. But they don't make a sound. They—they're nice, aren't they?"

He stood a little away from her to look up into her face. "Do you remember—in the song—'the world in solemn stillness lay?'" he asked her, but he knew she remembered.

The starlight showed him clear, his honest little-boy eyes wide, fixed trustingly on his mother's. He was deeply moved. But calm. This had come to him while he was still so young that he could be calmed by his mother's being with him. He had not known that he had an inner sanctuary. Now he stood in it, awe-struck at his first sight of beauty. And opened the door to his mother.

As naturally as he breathed, he put into his mother's hands the pure rounded pearl of a shared joy. "I thought I heard them singing—sort of," he told her.

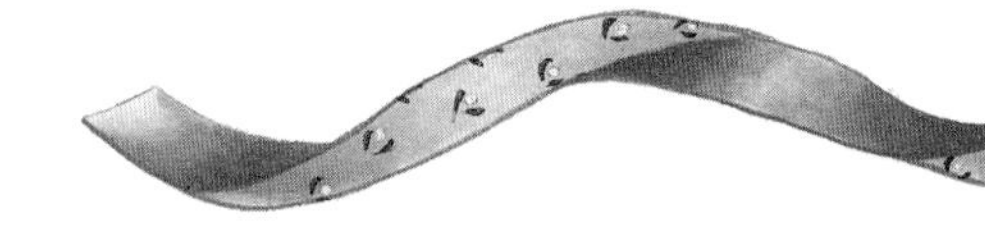

Christmas Eve

BEATRICE BRANCH

Tonight some magic sets my feet
Upon a starlit village street.
Trudging up the snowy road,
I sense a gaiety, bestowed
By that expectancy I knew
When youth and I kept rendezvous
With Christmastide. Candles, bright
Against the frosted pane, invite
Me home. The welcoming "hello"
Of loved ones brings a warming glow.

That special corner by the stair
Is livened by a spruce made fair
With ropes of popcorn, candy canes,
Iced gingermen, and paper chains.
Before the bedtime hour has rung,
Familiar carols have been sung
And Grandpa, once again, has told
Of the Messiah born of old.

Holding fast reality,
With gratefulness I turn the key
Within the lock that holds the past
To count the blessings there amassed.

"Christmas is a time of magic."

BESS MEREDITH

Topsham, Vermont
Dick Dietrich Photography

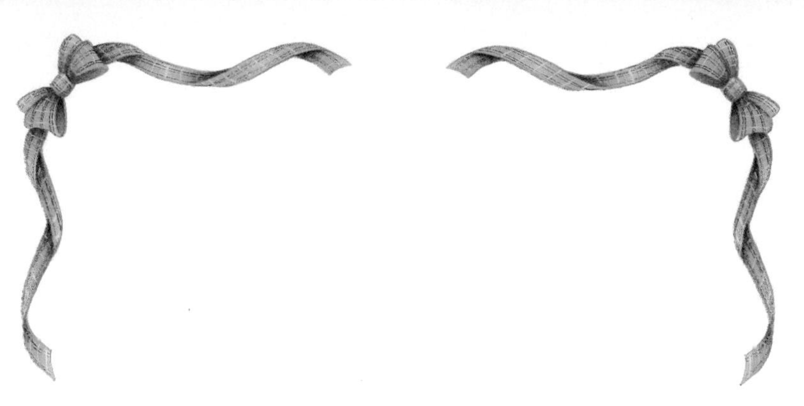

Christmas

ANTICIPATION

Presents stacked

beneath the tree,

Some for you,

some for me,

But we cannot peek,

you see,

This is Christmas!

Moonlight Funning
Jane Wooster Scott/Superstock

S
WHIZ
DEKE
ACE

Jolly Old St. Nicholas

TRADITIONAL

When the clock is striking twelve,
When I'm fast asleep,
Down the chimney broad and black,
With your pack you'll creep;
All the stockings you will find
Hanging in a row.
Mine will be the shortest one;
You'll be sure to know.

Johnny wants a pair of skates;
Susy wants a sled;
Nellie wants a picture book;
Yellow, blue, and red;
Now I think I'll leave to you
What to give the rest;
Choose for me, dear Santa Claus,
You will know the best.

"For Santa is a sprite that lives
In the heart that loves, in the heart that gives."

LEIGH HANES

Guessing Time

EDGAR A. GUEST

It's guessing time at our house;
Every evening after tea
We start guessing what old Santa's going
To leave us on our tree.
Everyone of us holds secrets
That the others try to steal
And that eyes and lips are plainly having
Trouble to conceal.
And a little lip that quivered just
A bit the other night
Was a sad and startling warning that
I mustn't guess it right.

"Guess what you'll get for Christmas!"
Is the cry that starts the fun.
And I answer: "Give the letter
With which the name's begun."
Oh, the eyes that dance around me
And the joyous faces there
Keep me nightly guessing wildly:
"Is it something I can wear?"
I implore them all to tell me
In a frantic sort of way
And pretend that I am puzzled,
Just to keep them feeling gay.

Oh, the wise and knowing glances
That across the table fly
And the winks exchanged with Mother,
That they think I never spy;
Oh, the whispered confidences
That are poured into her ear,
And the laughter gay that follows
When I try my best to hear!
Oh, the shouts of glad derision when
I bet that it's a cane,
And the merry answering chorus:
"No it's not. Just guess again!"

It's guessing time at our house,
And the fun is running fast,
And I wish somehow this contest
Of delight could always last.
For the love that's in their faces
And their laughter ringing clear
Is their dad's most precious present
When the Christmastime is near.
And soon as it is over,
When the tree is bare and plain,
I shall start in looking forward
To the time to guess again.

West End Holiday Home Tour
Winston Salem, North Carolina

A Letter from Santa Claus

ELEANOR ESTES

Rufus wanted a pony. In this he was no different from every other small boy. Every Christmas Rufus asked Santa Claus for one. In his letters to Santa Claus, a pony always topped the list. Oh, of course, he used to ask for other things too, a bicycle, a top, an engine, toy soldiers, a jack-knife, but the pony was what he wanted more than anything else in the world. He tried in his letters to point this out to Santa Claus. For instance, in one letter he put a gold star by the word "pony." In another he wrote "pony" in red crayon. Still Santa Claus didn't seem to catch on, and he never brought a pony. He brought other fine things, pea blowers, horns, drums, and Rufus was grateful for them; but they didn't answer that longing he had inside for a pony.

How did he get it into his head he wanted a pony? Well, one day a couple of years ago, when the Moffats were living in the yellow house on New Dollar Street, a man had come along leading a black and white pony. You could have your picture taken sitting on its back for ten cents. Mama said Rufus should have one taken. She would frame it and put it on the mantel. So the man picked Rufus up and set him on the pony's back and took his picture.

Then the man let Rufus ride the pony as far as Hughie Pudge's house. There, however, he had to get down and let Hughie Pudge get up, for he was going to have his picture taken too. Ever since that time when he had felt real pony flesh between his legs, Rufus had wanted a pony just terribly.

Last Christmas, Santa Claus had brought him a brown felt pony on wheels, all right for very small children perhaps, but certainly not the thing for him. After this experience Rufus decided he'd better add the word "ALIVE" after "pony."

This Christmas Mama said to the children, "Do not ask Santa Claus for too much this year because you know, there is a terrible war going on in Europe and Santa Claus will need an extra large amount of things for the Belgian children." So one evening, after the supper dishes had been cleared away, Jane and Rufus took pencil and paper to the kitchen table, pushed back the red-checked tablecloth, and wrote their letters to Santa Claus. Jane wrote:

Dear Santa Claus,
Please bring me:
Two-storied pencil box
Flexible flier sled
Box of paints
Princess and Curdie.

Then she stopped for a moment. She would like to say, "Please don't bring any material for a dress or anything to wear, or for practical's sake." But perhaps Santa Claus would not think that was polite, so she signed,

With love, Jane Moffat.

She looked over at Rufus's letter. "Have you finished?" she asked.

"Not quite," he answered. His tongue was between his teeth and he was working very hard. Jane watched him curiously for he was no longer writing but was drawing something on his letter with brown crayon.

"How many things you ask for?" he demanded presently.

"Four," said Jane.

"Four!" repeated Rufus. "I only ast for one," he announced with satisfaction. When he finally laid down his crayon, he held his letter up and surveyed it approvingly.

"Can I look at it?" asked Jane.

Looking at one another's letters to Santa Claus was usually an unheard-of procedure. They were for Santa's eyes only. But this letter Rufus was proud of and he pushed it over to Jane with a magnanimous gesture.

This was Rufus's letter:

DEAR Santy CLOS,
Pleez bring me a pony,
Alive.
RUFUS

"Gee, that's nice," approved Jane.

"Think he'll know what I mean?"

"Sure."

"Maybe I better add the words 'real one' under the picture just to make sure," said Rufus. So he carefully printed the words "REAL ONE" under his drawing and was convinced that now he had made it plain to Santa Claus what he wanted for Christmas. He and Jane took their letters to the kitchen stove, lifted the lid, and dropped them into the red hot coals. The draught whisked them up the chimney and the charred letters were gone.

"Funny he can read them when they are burned up like that," said Rufus.

"He just can," said Jane with finality.

Rufus went back to the kitchen table and wrote another letter with a picture of an "ALIVE" pony on it. This he gave to Mama to put in her bag and mail in the big post office tomorrow when she went to town.

"I'm sure he'll get one or the other of them," said Rufus.

Jane sat down before the kitchen fire to warm her toes. "Dear God," she prayed, "tell Santy Claus to bring him a pony." She could not bear to think of another Christmas Day with no pony for Rufus. . . .

Then she began thinking about what to give Mama this Christmas. Something especially lovely. What was the loveliest thing she could think of? She watched the sparkling coals and suddenly she had a wonderful idea. The gift should be a beautiful bag, brocaded and sparkling with gold and silver threads, all embroidered together into a gorgeous pattern. Yes! She had seen such a bag once in a store window on Chapel Street in town. Certainly that was the gift for Mama.

She called Joe and Rufus. She didn't call Sylvie because Sylvie already had all her presents wrapped and hidden on the top shelf of the pantry.

"How much money you got?" she asked them.

"What do you want to know for?" they both countered.

Jane told them about the bag. She painted it in glowing colors. "It'll be lovely. It'll be shiny all over," she ended up. Rufus and Joe were impressed. They liked the idea. Well now! A brocaded bag for Mama. That was something!

"Well, how much money have you got?" asked Jane. "Because I don't have enough just by myself. And this brockated bag'll be from the whole three of us."

Rufus disappeared in the closet under the stairs and came back with his old Prince Albert tobacco box he kept his treasures in. Among the bottle tops in it he found a few pennies, six in all. He dropped them in Jane's lap.

Joe put his hand in his pocket. He kept his money there, when he had any, like a grown man. Finally he pulled out two nickels and two pennies and dropped them into Jane's lap. Jane opened the little Chinese purse that Mama and Sylvie had brought her from New York's Chinatown. A nickel and four pennies fell out of this. Altogether it looked quite a pile. She scooped it up in the palm of her hand.

"Twenty-seven cents!" she announced with satisfaction, shaking the coins up and down, up and down.

"Will that buy one of those bags?" asked Joe incredulously.

"Oh, no," replied Jane scornfully. "They cost a dollar at least. I'm goin' to make this brockated bag."

"Supposin' you don't finish it before Christmas?" asked Joe. "Then I'll have nothin' for Mama."

"I'll finish it," said Jane positively. Again she painted the bag she would make in glowing terms, for she saw that their enthusiasm was lagging. She rolled the words lovingly on her tongue, gold threads, silver threads, cerise, peacock blue, threads of silk and satin . . . brocaded . . . Well, they were won over again.

"Tomorrow we'll go to Aberdeen's and get the things," she concluded, exhausted from all this persuading. . . .

The next day it was snowing very hard. It had begun in the middle of the night. Silently a soft, thick mantle had been laid over the earth and it was growing thicker by the minute. Jane and Joe and Rufus ran to the front window and looked out. Marvelous! The first deep snow of winter! They waved good-bye to Sylvie who was making her way with difficulty through the deep drifts.

"Where's she goin'?" asked Rufus.

"To the Parish House to rehearse for the Christmas tableau," said Jane. "Come on. Get ready to go to Aberdeen's and get the things."

"All right, let's go," said Rufus impatiently.

They put on their rubbers. "Mine leak," said Jane, looking at the holes in the heels and toes. "But never mind, Santy Claus," she breathed, "I don't care a thing about whole rubbers." Rubbers would be worse to see on Christmas morning than material for a dress. . . .

Out into the snow they ran. The whole world was white. Soon they looked like snow men. "Boy, oh, boy, I'll have plenty of shoveling to do when we get back," said Joe.

Although they could walk on the sidewalk, most of which had been cleared by the snowplow, they preferred to walk through the deep snow on the side of the pavements. They sank into the soft snow as far as their knees. This was good fun. After a while Jane said, "We better hurry. And anyway, my chilblains are itching me. And I want to get home and start that bag."

At last they reached Aberdeen's department store, the only large store in Cranbury. . . . Mrs. Aberdeen herself, dressed in many sweaters and a black apron, came to wait on them. She had a pencil stuck in the bun of her hair, a tape measure around her neck, and a pair of scissors strung on a black silk ribbon dangling from her bosom. Mrs. Aberdeen looked more like Madame-the-bust than anyone else in Cranbury.

"What do you want, children?" she asked briskly.

Jane looked at her, wondering how to begin. It was clear that Mrs. Aberdeen was not going to guess "brockated bag" just by looking at the three Moffats.

"Well, speak up," she said, more briskly still. "A spool of thread? A yard of elastic? Garters? Buttons?"

"No," said Jane. "We, that is, I, that is, we're all giving it, but I'm making it, want to make a bag for Mama for Christmas."

"Oh, well . . . I see . . . well, now, how much money can you spend?"

Jane opened the little Chinese purse and the nickels and pennies rolled out on the counter.

"Twenty-seven cents," said Jane. "And I want to 'broider the bag."

"Yes. Well, twenty-seven cents can't buy much."

"A brockated bag," Jane breathed, but Mrs. Aberdeen didn't hear her.

"Here's a nice piece of goods you can have for that money," said Mrs. Aberdeen, holding up a piece of blue calico.

"I want to 'broider the bag," Jane repeated faintly.

Mrs. Aberdeen pulled out a skein of white embroidery cotton. "There," she said kindly. "I'm sure that will make a very nice bag."

"These things don't shine. Something is wrong," thought Jane, almost sobbing. But she paid the money and Mrs. Aberdeen deftly wrapped up the cloth and the embroidery thread in crackling green paper. With a real, bought package under her arm, Jane felt better. Then, too, the plain blue calico was out of sight and her vision of the brocaded bag returned in full force. It danced before her, a lovely elusive thing that quickened her pace. Joe and Rufus practically had to run to keep up with her.

"Will that be the brockated bag?" panted Joe.

"Wait and see," replied Jane with such an air of confidence that any doubts that Joe and Rufus might have had were cast immediately to the winds. By the time they reached home, the brocaded bag was again the beautiful teasing vision they all had had.

Mama was in the kitchen, so they unwrapped the green package in the little green and white parlor with eager fingers. They would not have been surprised had the blue calico changed into a brocaded bag on the way home. However, the blue calico was still blue calico, though it was obvious from Jane's joyful spirits that she would have this transformed into the other lovely thing in no time.

During the next few days, Jane worked hard on the bag. She cut it out and sewed it up, every stitch by hand. She embroidered "MAMA" on one side of it with the white embroidery thread. On the other, she embroidered a daisy. When she finished it, she held it up and surveyed it with satisfaction. The brocaded bag! She saw it flash and sparkle and gleam with different shining colors. It was the very bag she had seen in the big store window in town.

In excitement she called Joe and Rufus in to see the finished bag. She dangled it before them, walked mincingly with it on her arm as elegant ladies do, thinking perhaps she looked like Mrs. Stokes.

"Is that a brockated bag?" they asked wonderingly.

"Yes!" said Jane. "Isn't it lovely?" And she

walked up to the mirror to look at herself with the pretty thing. Her eyes fell on the bag. What they saw there was a very plain blue calico bag with a crooked "MAMA" embroidered on one side and a humped-back daisy on the other. She looked down at the real bag hanging on her arm. The fair vision of the brocaded bag vanished completely and forever. She fell silent. The boys said nothing. After all, they had never seen a brocaded bag. In a while Jane said thoughtfully, "It will be good to keep buttons in."

They wrapped it up and made a card for it, "To Mama, with love from Joe, Rufus, and Jane," and hid it where Mama would not be able to find it.

At last it was Christmas Eve. The four Moffats were making decorations for the tree, angels of gold and silver paper, baskets for candy and cookies, chains of colored paper, cornucopias for popcorn. The kitchen table was quite covered with scraps of paper and sticky with flour-and-water paste which Rufus had dabbed around by mistake. . . . Sylvie and Mama were going to help Santa Claus out by having the tree trimmed before he came late tonight. At present they were busy making the spiced Santa Claus cookies for the tree. How good they did smell!

"It is time now to hang your stockings," said Mama.

The four of them, even Sylvie, tore off to their rooms to find stockings that didn't have any holes in them so none of the good things would fall out of the heel or toe. They tacked these onto the wainscoting behind the kitchen stove, right handy for Santa Claus.

Now there was really nothing to do but go to bed. Rufus and Janey went first. They stripped off their clothes before the kitchen fire. They put on their outing flannel bed-socks and nightclothes and raced noisily up the stairs to bed.

But not to sleep! Not yet! They talked and laughed, smothering their giggles under the bedclothes. They whispered, "What do you think Santy Claus will bring us?"

"Let's stay awake all night and watch for Santy Claus," said Rufus.

"What are Mama and Sylvie so mysterious about?" Jane asked.

"What do you think Santy will bring?" Rufus asked this for the hundredth time, although there was really little doubt in his mind. Had he not written Santa Claus the same letter every night for a week, telling him to bring a real live pony, even showing by drawings exactly what he meant? Goodness knows how many of these letters had found their way to Santa Claus. So many probably that Rufus had grown rather worried at the last and varied his letter to read,

> DEAR SANTY,
> Please bring me a live pony. ONE is plenty.
> RUFUS.

"Goodness," he chuckled, "if Santy brought a pony for every letter I wrote! . . . But I guess he'll know better than that."

In spite of themselves, they began to grow sleepy. . . . Jane stayed awake, however. Her chilblains itched her. But she wasn't thinking about them so much. She was thinking about Rufus and that pony he expected.

"He certainly does want that pony," she thought. "He wants that pony harder than I have ever wanted anything."

And this year he was so positive that Santa would bring one. Nevertheless, Jane had a sinking feeling in her stomach that Christmas morning would come and there just would not be a pony for Rufus. What should she do? His disappointment would be more than she could bear. "Something ought to be done," she worried, "but what?" . . .

For a long time Jane lay there. Supposing she stayed awake this year and listened for Santa Claus? A word in his ear about the pony might work wonders. Other years she had meant to do this, but somehow morning had always come and the stockings had been filled as by magic and she would realize that she had gone to sleep and missed Santa Claus after all. He had come in the middle of the night. This year would be different though. She would stay awake—yes, she would. . . . Now all she had to do was to listen for Santa Claus. . . . She must stay awake and . . .

In telling Nancy about this night later, Jane was positive she had stayed awake. Positive that just as the clock in the sitting room downstairs struck twelve, Santa Claus had stood beside her bed and gently turned her over. His frosty beard had even brushed her cheek. And he had whispered something in her ear. But just as she was about to speak to him, he had vanished and the sleigh bells tinkled off in the distance.

She sat up in bed. Sylvie was sleeping peacefully. Santa Claus had gone. Of that she was sure. Oh, why had he not waited for her to speak? Softly she crept out of bed, felt her way past the chiffonier into the hall, and stole down the creaking stairs to the kitchen. She was grateful for the faint light that shone from the kitchen stove. Finding the matches, she struck one. Catherine-the-cat's eyes shone green and examined her with keen disapproval. Paying no attention to her, Jane glanced swiftly behind the stove. There the four stockings hung, bulging now. Yes, that proved it. Santa had been here just now and had come to her side to give her some message.

She glanced around the room and peeked into the little parlor where the Christmas tree was shining. There was no pony about. That was certain. She tiptoed to the back window and pressed her face against the pane. The moon shone over the white snow, making a light almost as bright as day. If there had been a pony out there, she would know it. There just wasn't any pony and there was no use hoping for it any longer. That was why Santa had come to her bedside. He knew she was awake and waiting and he had a good reason for not bringing the pony, and that's what he had wanted to tell her. What was the reason? She thought for a moment. Then she knew. She lighted another match, found a piece of brown wrapping paper and a pencil. Crouching on the floor near the stove she wrote,

> Dear Rufus,
> All the ponies are at the war.
> Your friend, Santy Claus.

She tucked this note in the top of Rufus's stocking and went back to bed. Shivering, she pressed her cold self against Sylvie and fell sound asleep.

The next thing she knew, Sylvie was shaking her and shaking her and screaming, "Merry Christmas, Merry Christmas!" Jane jumped out of bed, pulled a blanket around her, danced wildly out of the room screaming "Merry Christmas, Merry Christmas!" Mama gave them each a sweet hug and a kiss and said, "Merry Christmas everybody." The whole house echoed and Catherine-the-cat chased her tail for the first time in five and a half years.

They grabbed their stockings and raced back to bed with them, for the house was still bitterly cold. A sudden yell from Rufus interrupted everything.

"Whoops!" he shouted. "Whoops! Listen to this! Mama! Listen! I've had a letter from Santy Claus." Rufus jumped out of bed and tore through the house like a cyclone, the others following him.

"Listen to this," he said again, where they were finally collected before the kitchen fire. "'Dear Rufus,' it says. 'Dear Rufus, All the ponies are at the war,' and it's signed 'Your friend, Santy Claus!' Imagine a letter from Santy Claus himself!"

Mama put on her glasses and examined the note carefully. "H-m-m-m," she said.

"Gee," said Rufus, "wait till I show this to Eddie Bangs. He's always boastin' of his autograph collection. He's got President Taft, Mayor Harley, Chief Mulligan. But he ain't got Santy Claus."

Jane could see that having a letter from Santa Claus himself softened considerably Rufus's disappointment in not getting a real live pony.

When calm was somewhat restored, the gifts were taken from the tree. These were some of the most exciting moments: When Mama opened her "brockated bag" and said, "This will be elegant to keep buttons in"; when Rufus opened his toy village—houses, trees, grocery boys on bicycles, delivery men with horses and wagons, firemen and fire engines, a postman, a policeman and a milkman—yes, a complete village to lay out with streets and parks; when Jane opened her miniature grocery store, with tiny boxes of real cocoa and salt, sacks of sugar and the smallest jars of real honey; when Sylvie opened a huge box and drew out a fluffy white dress Mama had secretly made for her first ball, the Junior-Senior promenade; and when Joe opened a long, slim package that had a shining clarinet in it! "Boy, oh, boy," was all he could say.

But now it was time for Sylvie to go to church to take her part in the Christmas tableau. Of course all the Moffats were going to watch her and join in the beautiful Christmas carols. Before they left, however, Mama gathered them all around the tree and they sang:

> "Hark! The herald angels sing,
> Glory to the newborn King.
> Peace on earth and mercy mild,
> God and sinners reconciled!"

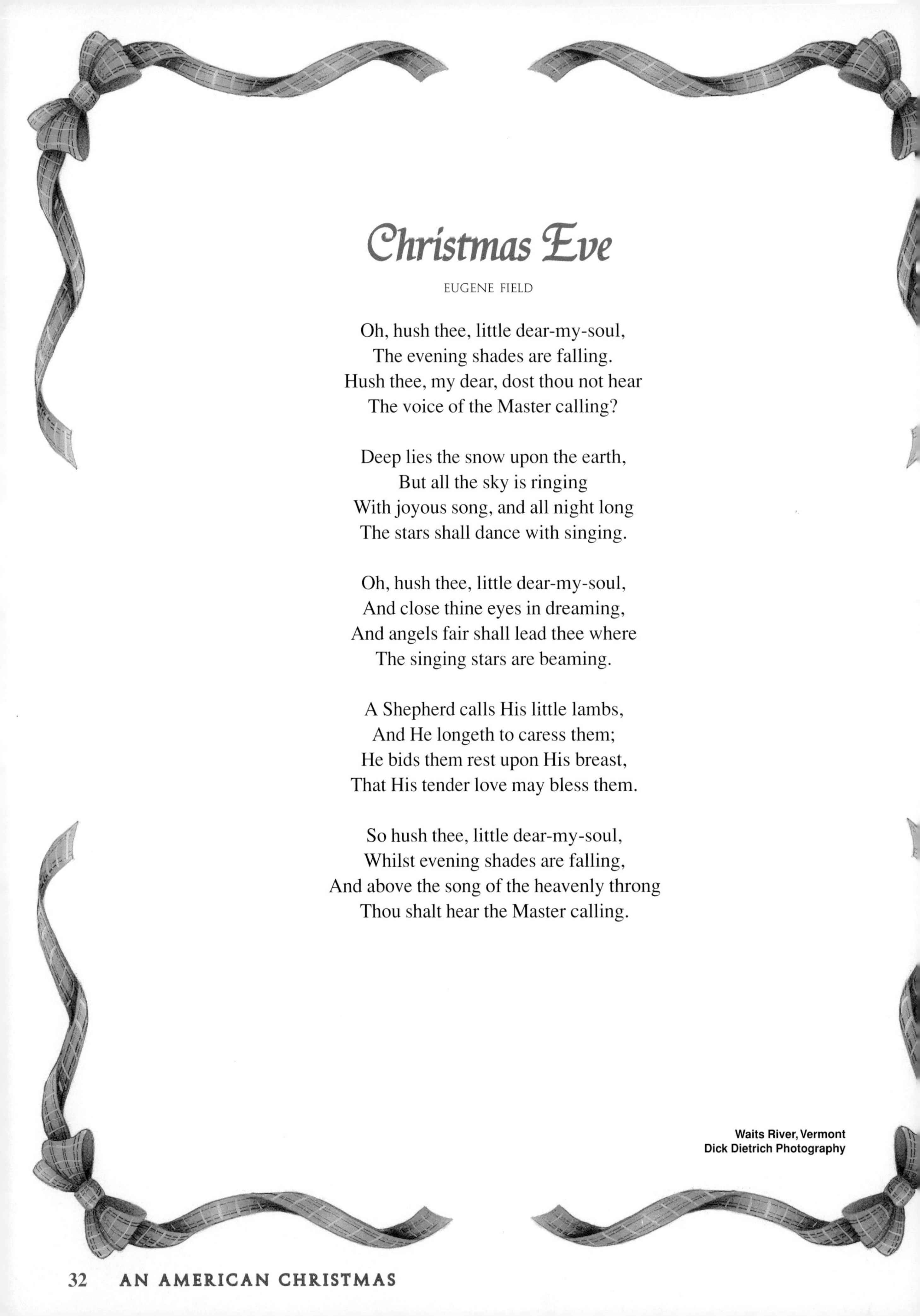

Christmas Eve

EUGENE FIELD

Oh, hush thee, little dear-my-soul,
The evening shades are falling.
Hush thee, my dear, dost thou not hear
The voice of the Master calling?

Deep lies the snow upon the earth,
But all the sky is ringing
With joyous song, and all night long
The stars shall dance with singing.

Oh, hush thee, little dear-my-soul,
And close thine eyes in dreaming,
And angels fair shall lead thee where
The singing stars are beaming.

A Shepherd calls His little lambs,
And He longeth to caress them;
He bids them rest upon His breast,
That His tender love may bless them.

So hush thee, little dear-my-soul,
Whilst evening shades are falling,
And above the song of the heavenly throng
Thou shalt hear the Master calling.

Waits River, Vermont
Dick Dietrich Photography

Once on Christmas

DOROTHY THOMPSON

It is Christmas Eve—the festival that belongs to mothers and fathers and children, all over the so-called Western world. It's not a time to talk about situations, or conditions, or reactions, or people who emerge briefly into the news. My seven-year-old son asked me this evening to tell him what Christmas was like when I was a little girl, before people came home for Christmas in airplanes, thirty odd years ago. And so I told him this:

A long, long time ago, when your mother was your age, and not nearly as tall as you, she lived with her mother, and father, and younger brother, and little sister, in a Methodist parsonage, in Hamburg, New York. It was a tall wooden house, with a narrow verandah on the side, edged with curly-cues of woodwork at the top, and it looked across a lawn at the church where father preached every Sunday morning and evening. In the back yard there were old Baldwin and Greening apple trees, and a wonderful, wonderful barn. But that is another story. The village now has turned into a suburb of the neighboring city of Buffalo, and fathers who work there go in and out every day on the trains and buses, but then it was just a little country town, supported by the surrounding farms. . . .

For weeks before Christmas we were very, very busy. Mother was busy in the kitchen, cutting up citron and sorting out raisins and clarifying suet for the Christmas pudding—and shooing all of us out of the room when we crept in to snatch a raisin, or a bit of kernel from the butter-nuts that my little brother was set to cracking on the woodshed floor with an old-fashioned flat-iron.

I would lock myself into my little bedroom to bend over a handkerchief that I was hemstitching for my mother. It is very hard to hemstitch when you are seven years old, and the thread would knot, and break, and then one would have to begin again, with a little rough place where one had started over. I'm afraid the border of that handkerchief was just one succession of knots and starts.

The homemade presents were only a tiny part of the work! There was the Christmas tree! Mr. Heist, from my father's Armor parish, had brought it from his farm, a magnificent hemlock that touched the ceiling. We were transported with admiration, but what a tree to trim! For there was no money to buy miles of tinsel and boxes of colored glass balls.

But in the pantry was a huge stone jar of popcorn. When school was over in the afternoons, we all gathered in the back parlor, which was the family sitting room. The front parlor was a cold place, where portraits of John Wesley and Frances Willard hung on the walls, and their eyes, I remember, would follow a naughty child accusingly around the room. The sofas in that room were of walnut, with roses and grapes carved on their backs, just where they'd stick into your back if you fidgeted in them, and were covered with horse-hair which was slippery when it was new, and tickly when it was old. But that room was given over to visits from the local tycoons who sometimes contributed to the church funds and couples who came to be married.

The back parlor was quite, quite different. It had an ingrain carpet on the floor, with patterns of maple leaves, and white muslin curtains at the windows, and an assortment of chairs contributed by the parsonage committee. A Morris chair, I remember, and some rockers, and a fascinating cabinet which was a desk and a bookcase, and a chest of drawers, and a mirror, all in one.

In this room there was a round iron stove, a very jolly stove, a cozy stove that winked at you with its red isin-glass eyes. On top of this stove was a round iron plate; it was flat, and a wonderful place to pop corn. There was a great copper kettle, used for making maple syrup, and we shook the popper on the top of the stove—first I shook, until my arm was tired, and then Willard shook, until he was tired, and even the baby shook. The corn popped, and we poured it into the kettle and emptied the kettle, and poured it full again, until there was a whole barrel full of popcorn, as white and fluffy as the snow that carpeted the lawn between the parsonage and the church.

Then we each got a darning needle, a big one, and a ball of string. We strung the popcorn into long, long ropes to hang upon the tree. But that was only half of it! There were stars to be cut out of kindergarten paper, red and green, and silver, and gold, and walnuts to be wrapped in gold paper, or painted with gold paint out of the paint box that I had been given for my birthday. One got the paint into one's fingernails, and it smelled like bananas. And red apples to be polished, because a shiny apple makes a brave show on a tree. And when it was all finished, it was Christmas Eve.

For Christmas Eve we all wore our best clothes. Baby in a little challis dress as blue as her eyes, and I had a new pinafore of Swiss lawn that my Aunt Margaret had sent me from England. We waited, breathless, in the front parlor while the candles were lit.

Then my mother sat at the upright piano in a rose-red cashmere dress and played, and my father sang, in his lovely, pure, gay, tenor voice:

"It came upon the midnight clear
That glorious song of old,
From angels bending near the earth
To touch their harps of gold."

And then we all marched in. It is true that we had decorated the tree ourselves, and knew intimately everything on it, but it shone in the dark room like an angel, and I could see the angels bending down, and it was so beautiful that one could hardly bear it. We all cried, "Merry Christmas!" and kissed each other.

There were bundles under the tree, most alluring bundles! But they didn't belong to Christmas Eve. They were for the morning. Before the morning came, three little children would sit sleepily in the pews of their father's church and hear words drowsily, and shift impatiently, and want to go to sleep in order to wake up very, very early!

And wake up early we did! The windows were still gray, and, oh, how cold the room was! The church janitor had come over at dawn to stoke the hot air furnace in the parsonage, but at its best it only heated the rooms directly above it, and the upstairs depended on grates in the floor and the theory that heat rises. We shuddered out of our beds, trembling with cold and excitement, and into our clothes, which, when I was a little girl, were very complicated affairs indeed. First, a long fleece-lined union suit, and then a ferris waist dripping with buttons, then the cambric drawers edged with embroidery, and a flannel petticoat handsome with scallops, and another petticoat of cambric and embroidery, just for show, and over that a gay plaid dress, and a dainty pinafore. What polishing of cheeks, and what brushing of hair and then a grand tumble down the stairs into the warm, cozy back parlor.

Presents! There was my beloved Miss Jam-up with a brand new head! Miss Jam-up was once a sweet little doll, dears, who had become badly battered about the face in the course of too affectionate ministrations, and here she was again, with a new head altogether and new clothes, and eyes that open and shut. Scarves and mittens from my mother's lively fingers. A doll house made from a wooden cracker box and odds and ends of wall paper, with furniture cut from stiff cardboard—and that was mother's work, too. And a new woolen dress, and new pinafores!

Under the tree was a book: *The Water Babies*, by Charles Kingsley. *To my beloved daughter Dorothy.*

Books meant sheer magic. There were no automobiles—none for Methodist ministers, in those days. No moving pictures. No radio. But inside the covers of books was everything, everything, that exists outside in the world today. Lovely, lovely words of poetry that slipped like colored beads along a string; tales of rose-red cities, half as old as time. All that men can imagine, and construct, and make others imagine.

One couldn't read the book now. But here it lay, the promise of a perfect afternoon. Before one could get at it, one would go into the dining room. And what a dinner! This Christmas there was turkey—with best wishes from one of my father's parishioners. And the pudding, steaming, and with two kinds of sauce. And no one to say, "No, dear, I think one helping is enough."

We glutted ourselves, we distended ourselves, we ate ourselves into a coma, so that we all had to lie down and have a nap. Then, lying before the stove, propped on my elbows, I opened the covers of my Christmas book. . . .

What a book! It wasn't just a story. There was poetry in it. The words of the poems sang in my head, so that after all these years I can remember them. . . .

The little girl lay and dreamed that all the world was wide and beautiful, filled only with hearts as warm and hands as tender, and spirits as generous as the only ones she had ever known . . . when she was seven years old.

I wish you all a Merry Christmas!
I wish us all a world as kind as a
child can imagine it!

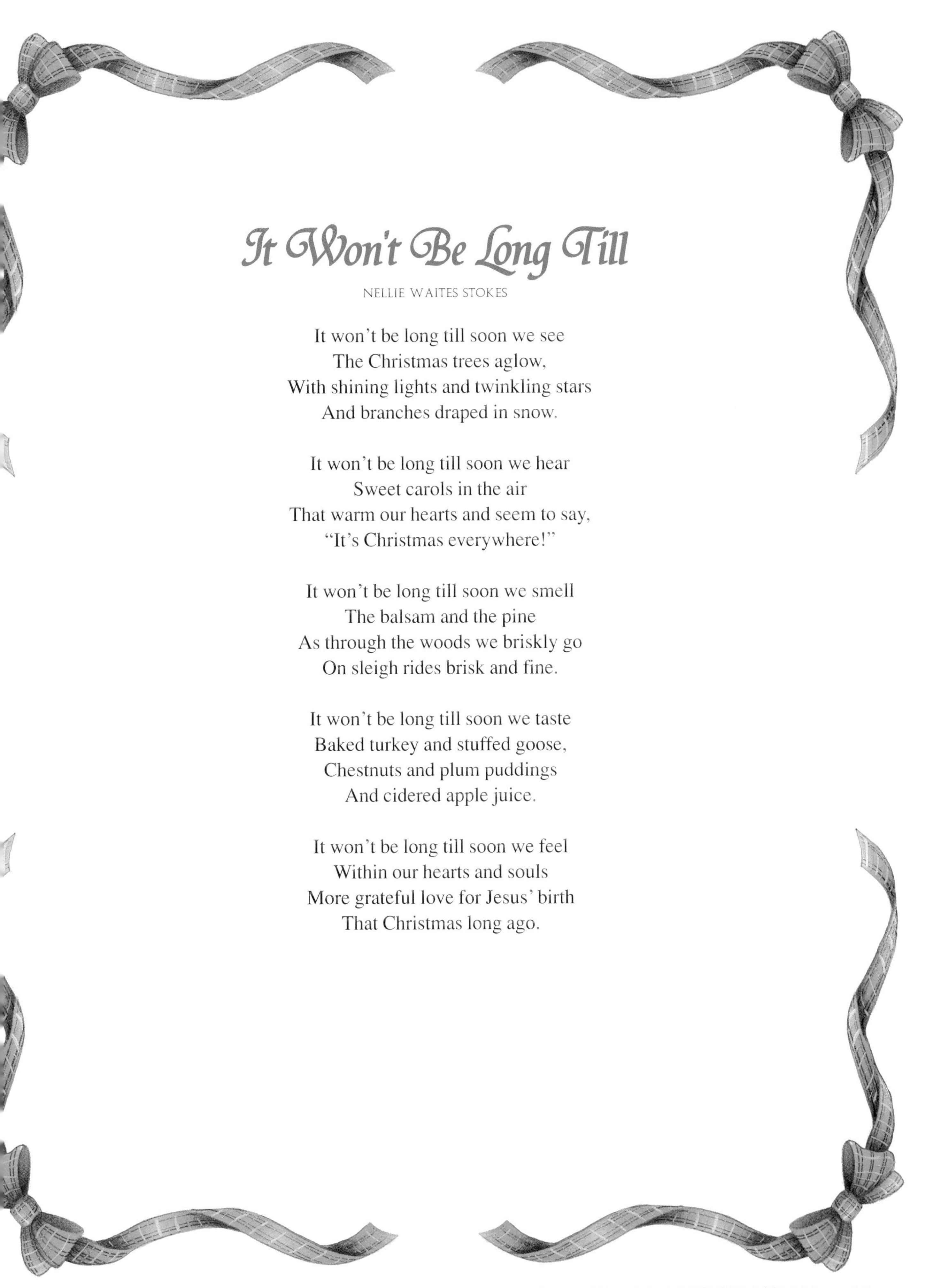

It Won't Be Long Till

NELLIE WAITES STOKES

It won't be long till soon we see
The Christmas trees aglow,
With shining lights and twinkling stars
And branches draped in snow.

It won't be long till soon we hear
Sweet carols in the air
That warm our hearts and seem to say,
"It's Christmas everywhere!"

It won't be long till soon we smell
The balsam and the pine
As through the woods we briskly go
On sleigh rides brisk and fine.

It won't be long till soon we taste
Baked turkey and stuffed goose,
Chestnuts and plum puddings
And cidered apple juice.

It won't be long till soon we feel
Within our hearts and souls
More grateful love for Jesus' birth
That Christmas long ago.

Christmas Greetings

YEARLY MESSAGES

I remember the excitement of each season's first Christmas card. I always made it my job to walk the long driveway to the mailbox each afternoon in December, through cold and snow, with our Labrador retriever, Barron, following along by my side, a jingling bell on his bright red collar. I was waiting for that first flash of green or red, the first color in the otherwise monotonous white and gray envelopes of the daily delivery.

At home, I strung the cards along the mantel; in some years the line of brightly colored cards reached from one wall to the opposite. My brothers and I liked to try and guess the sender by his card. Mrs. Thomas always sent birds; the MacDonalds always chose horses; Gramma always sent us a religious card with a manger scene on the front. Today, the joys of a simple Christmas card may seem overshadowed by the many spectacular sights and sounds of the holidays, but I still cherish each card that finds its way to my mailbox, both for the message it brings and for the memories it rekindles.—R. M. Cairns

Early twentieth-century, American Christmas cards. Superstock.

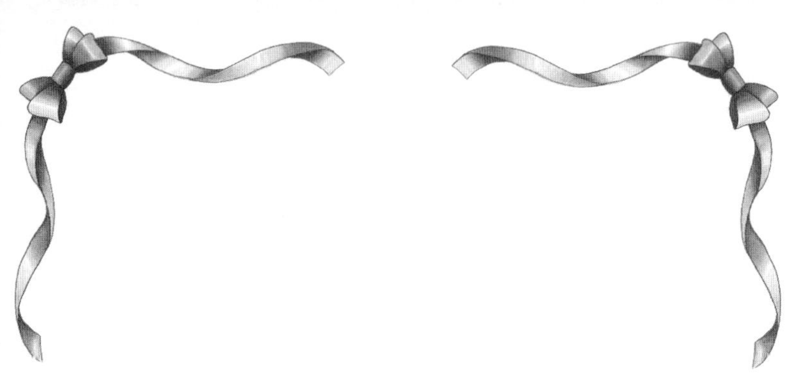

Christmas DECORATIONS

Festive trees and

child's delight,

Carols ringing

through the night,

Frosted panes aglow

with light—

This is Christmas!

Holiday Sleigh Ride
Jane Wooster Scott/Superstock

CERVA
PALMER
Holiday Sleigh Ride
Wooster Scott

Jehovah Hallelujah

SPIRITUAL

This Is Christmas

BETH EDWARDS

Blazing hearths and drifting snow,
Holly wreaths and mistletoe,
Yuletide greetings, candle glow—
This is Christmas!

Festive trees and child's delight,
Carols ringing through the night,
Frosted panes aglow with light—
This is Christmas!

Presents stacked beneath the tree,
Some for you, some for me,
But we cannot peek, you see,
This is Christmas!

Children's happy voices sing
"Glory to the newborn King!"
While the church bells gaily ring—
This is Christmas!

Home they come from far and near,
Those whom family ties hold dear;
Laughing love and wholesome cheer—
This is Christmas!

Ancient tidings told again,
"Peace on earth, good will toward men!"
Precious now as they were then—
This is Christmas!

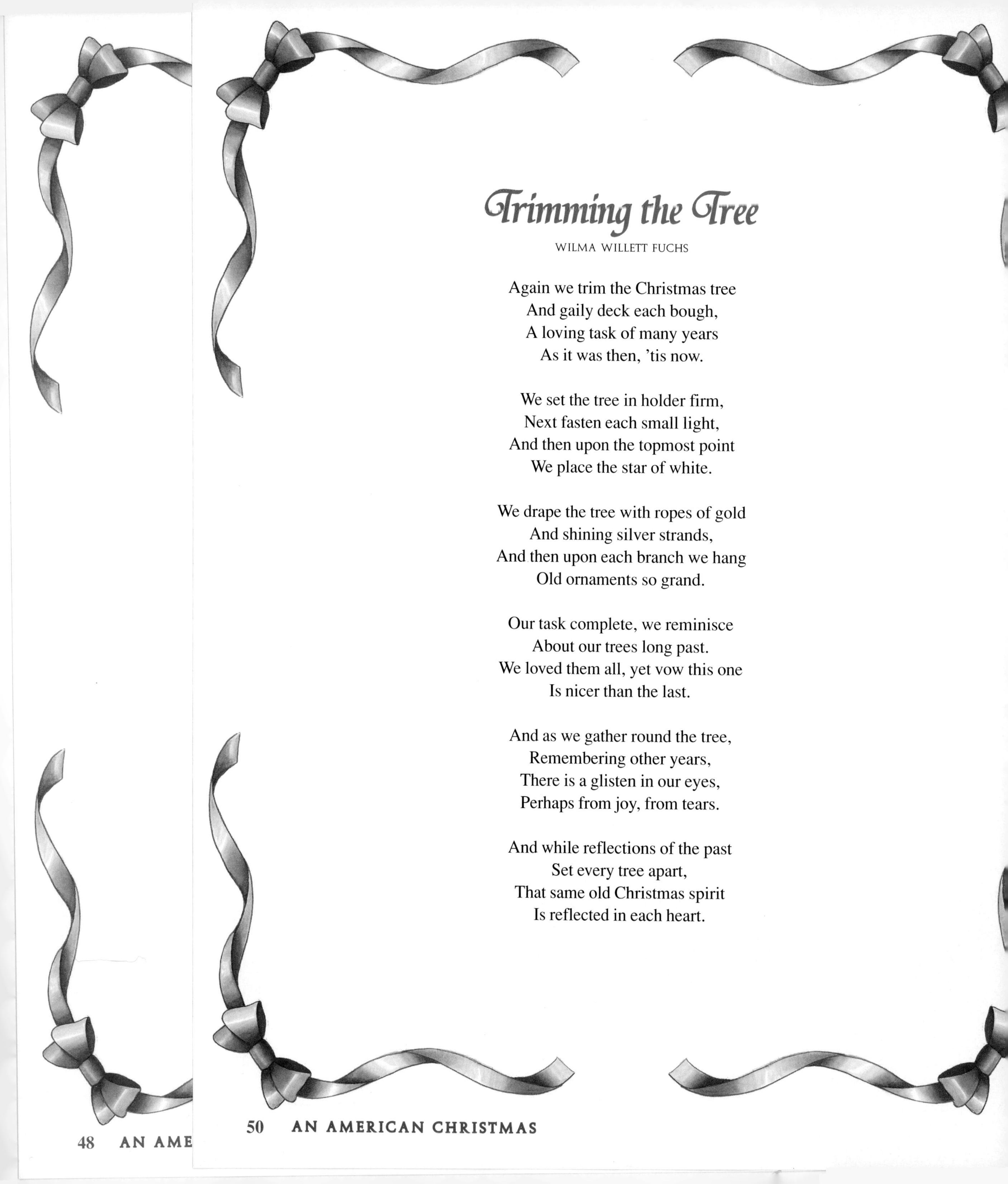

Trimming the Tree

WILMA WILLETT FUCHS

Again we trim the Christmas tree
And gaily deck each bough,
A loving task of many years
As it was then, 'tis now.

We set the tree in holder firm,
Next fasten each small light,
And then upon the topmost point
We place the star of white.

We drape the tree with ropes of gold
And shining silver strands,
And then upon each branch we hang
Old ornaments so grand.

Our task complete, we reminisce
About our trees long past.
We loved them all, yet vow this one
Is nicer than the last.

And as we gather round the tree,
Remembering other years,
There is a glisten in our eyes,
Perhaps from joy, from tears.

And while reflections of the past
Set every tree apart,
That same old Christmas spirit
Is reflected in each heart.

Christmas JOURNEYS

Home they come from

far and near,

Those whom family

ties hold dear;

Laughing love and

wholesome cheer—

This is Christmas!

Auld Lang Syne at the Golden Nugget Inn
Jane Wooster Scott/Superstock

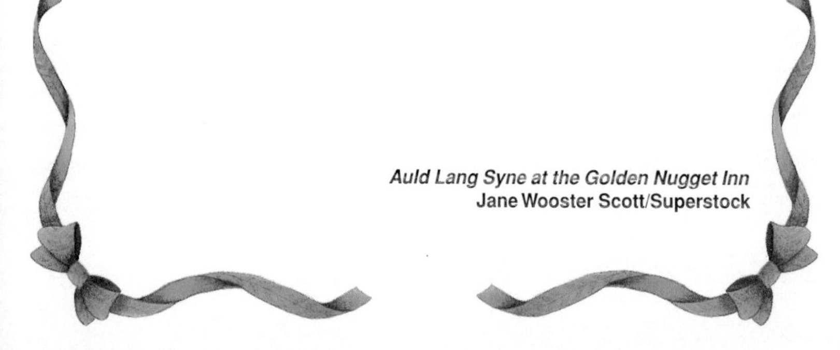

WELCOME 1907
HAPPY NEW YEAR
GOLDEN NUGGET INN
Auld Lang Syne At The Golden Nugget I
Wooster Scott

I Wonder as I Wander

WORDS AND MUSIC BY JOHN JACOB NILES

poor on - 'ry peo - ple like you and like
high from God's heav - en, a star's light did
all of God's an - gels in heav'n for to
poor on - 'ry peo - ple like you and like
I; I won - der as I wan - der out
fall, And the prom - ise of a - ges it
sing, He sure - ly could have it, 'cause
I; I won - der as I wan - der out
1.2.3.
un - der the sky.
then did re - call.
He was the King.
2. When
3. If
4. I
4.
un - der the
sky.

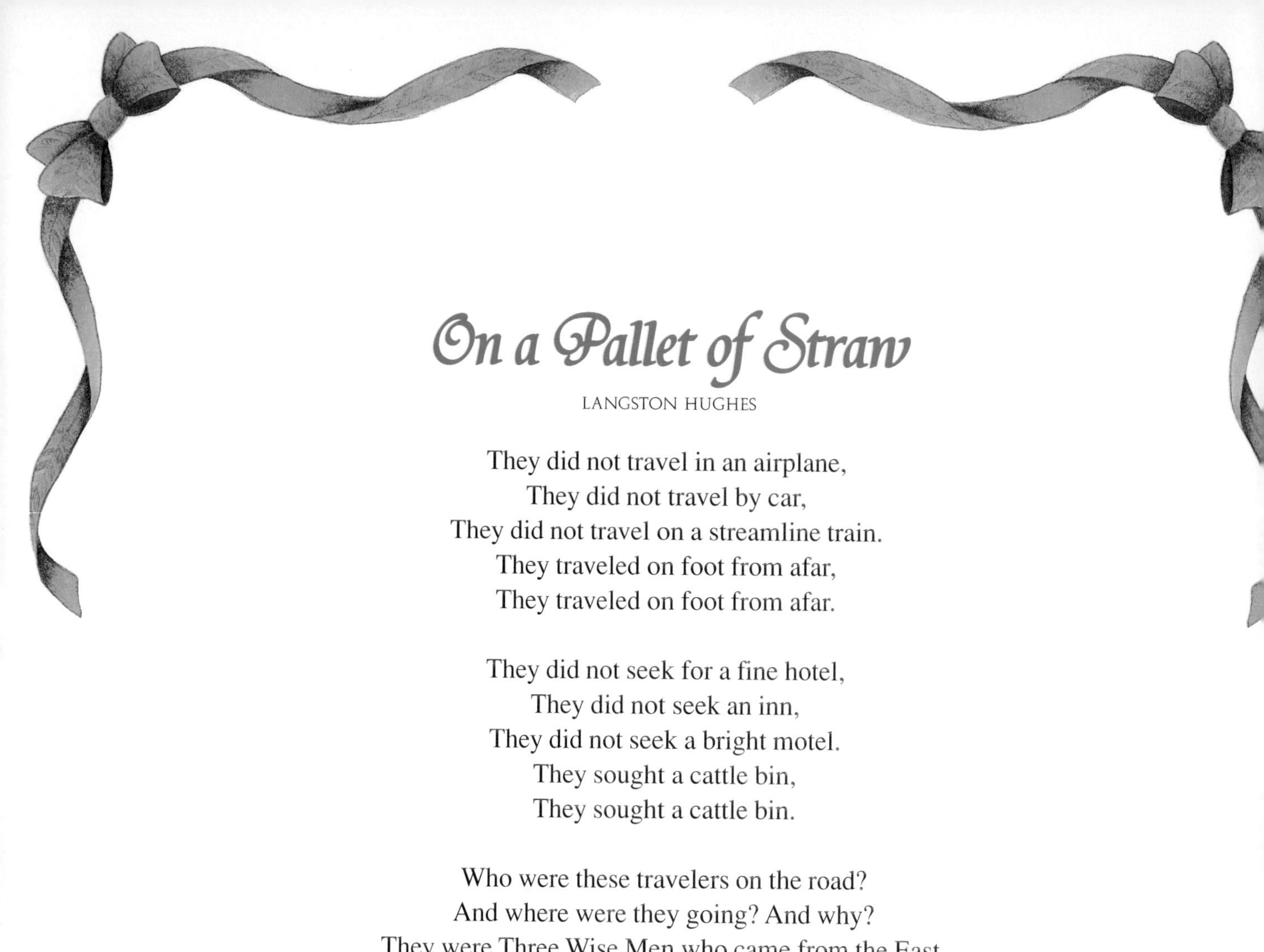

On a Pallet of Straw

LANGSTON HUGHES

They did not travel in an airplane,
They did not travel by car,
They did not travel on a streamline train.
They traveled on foot from afar,
They traveled on foot from afar.

They did not seek for a fine hotel,
They did not seek an inn,
They did not seek a bright motel.
They sought a cattle bin,
They sought a cattle bin.

Who were these travelers on the road?
And where were they going? And why?
They were Three Wise Men who came from the East,
And they followed a star in the sky,
A star in the sky.

What did they find when they got to the barn?
What did they find near the stall?
What did they find on a pallet of straw?
They found there the Lord of all!
They found the Lord of all!

***"O Father, may that holy star
Grow every year more bright
And send its glorious beams
To fill the world with light."***

WILLIAM CULLEN BRYANT

Jericho, Vermont
Superstock

Christmas Travels

JOURNEYS TO HEARTHSIDES NEAR AND FAR

Two days before Christmas we would pack up all of our gifts; our warmest coats, hats, and mittens; our ice skates and sled; and a supply of home-baked cookies and pile into the car for the eight-hour drive to my grandparents' farm in New Hampshire. We visited the farm several times a year—in the spring we would help plant the garden, in the heat of the summer we would swim in the lake and sleep on the screened porch, in the autumn we would pitch in during harvest—but Christmas was special; awaiting us in the farmhouse was an endless supply of cousins, candy, and cookies, and special packages under the tree, and on Christmas Eve there was caroling on the village green and midnight service at St. Andrew's. Even the drive, which could be long and uncomfortable, was a thrill at Christmas. That thrill remains; although my grandparents' farm is no longer my destination, I still love to travel at Christmastime. Every city, town, and village is somebody's home, somebody's special Christmas destination, and has something unique to offer the Christmas traveler.—Katharine Soucy

A Moravian band in Old Salem, North Carolina forms the sounds of the season.

Courtesy of Winston-Salem Convention & Visitors Bureau.

Over 400,000 tiny lights create the winter wonderland at Temple Square in Salt Lake City, Utah.

Courtesy of Salt Lake Convention and Visitors Bureau.

Teton Village in Jackson Hole, Wyoming, lights up the town square to celebrate the holidays.

Courtesy of Wyoming Division of Tourism.

he River Walk Holiday Parade is a favorite
vent of the season in San Antonio, Texas.
ourtesy of San Antonio Convention and Visitors Bureau.

The lights surrounding the antler arches illuminate the town square in Jackson Hole, Wyoming.
Courtesy of Wyoming Division of Tourism.

Liberty Hall Plantation in Kenansville, North Carolina, boasts festive decor for the holidays.
Courtesy of Duplin County Tourism.

The world-renowned Mormon Tabernacle Choir in Salt Lake City, Utah, presents an inspiring program of Christmas music as they have done for over a century.
Courtesy of Salt Lake Convention and Visitors Bureau.

At Christmas the Heart Goes Home

MARJORIE HOLMES

At Christmas, all roads lead home. The filled planes, packed trains, overflowing buses, all speak eloquently of a single destination: *home.* Despite the crowding and the crushing, the delays, the confusion, we clutch our bright packages and beam our anticipation. We are like birds driven by an instinct we only faintly understand—the hunger to be with our own people.

If we are already snug by our own fireside surrounded by growing children, or awaiting the return of older ones who are away, then the heart takes a side trip. In memory we journey back to the Christmases of long ago. Once again we are curled into quivering balls of excitement, listening to the mysterious rustle of tissue paper and the tinkle of untold treasures as parents perform their magic on Christmas Eve. Or we recall the special Christmases that are like little landmarks in the life of a family.

One memory is particularly dear to me—a Christmas during the Great Depression when Dad was out of work and the rest of us were scattered, struggling to get through school or simply to survive. My sister Gwen and her schoolteacher husband, on his first job in another state, were expecting their first baby. My brother Harold, an aspiring actor, was traveling with a road show. I was a senior working my way through a small college five hundred miles away. My boss had offered me fifty dollars—a fortune!—just to keep the office open in the two weeks he and his wife would be gone.

"And boy, do I need the money. Mom, I know you'll understand," I wrote. I wasn't prepared for her brave if wistful reply. The other kids couldn't make it either. Except for my kid brother, Barney, she and Dad would be alone. "The house is going to seem empty, but don't worry, we'll be okay."

I did worry, though. Our first Christmas apart! And as the carols drifted up the stairs, as the corridors rang with the laughter and chatter of other girls packing up to leave, my misery deepened.

Then one night when the dorm was almost empty I had a long distance call. "Gwen!" I gasped. "What's wrong?" (Long distance usually meant an emergency back in those days.)

"Listen, Leon's got a new generator, and we think the old jalopy can make it home. I've wired Harold—if he can meet us halfway, he can ride with us. But don't tell the folks; we want to surprise them. Marj, you've just got to come, too."

"But I haven't got a dime for presents."

"Neither have we. Cut up a catalogue and bring pictures of all the goodies you'd buy if you could—and will someday!"

"I could do that, Gwen, but I just can't leave here now." When we hung up, I reached for the scissors. Furs and perfume. Wristwatches, clothes, cars—how all of us longed to lavish beautiful things on those we loved. Well, at least I could mail mine home—with IOUs.

I was still dreaming over this "wish list" when I was called to the phone again. It was my boss, saying he'd decided to close the office after all. My heart leaped up, for if it wasn't too late to catch a ride as far as Fort Dodge with the girl down the hall! I ran to pound on her door.

They already had a load, she said—but if I was willing to sit on somebody's lap . . . Her dad was downstairs waiting. I threw things into a suitcase, then rammed a hand down the torn lining of my coat sleeve so fast it emerged mittened, and I had to start over.

It was snowing as we piled into that heaterless car. We drove all night with the side curtains flapping, singing and hugging each other to keep warm. Not minding—how could we? We were going home!

"Marj!" Mother stood at the door, clutching her robe about her, silver-black hair spilling down her back, eyes large with alarm, then incredulous joy. "Oh . . . *Marj.*"

I'll never forget those eyes, or the feel of her arms around me, so soft and warm after the bitter cold. My feet felt frozen after that all-night drive, but they warmed up as my parents fed me and put me to bed. And when I woke up hours later, it was to the jangle of the sleigh bells Dad hung on the door each year. And voices. My kid brother shouting "Harold! Gwen!" The clamor of astonished greetings, the laughter, the kissing, the questions. And we all gathered around the kitchen table, the way we used to, recounting our adventures.

"I had to hitchhike clear to Peoria," my older brother scolded merrily. "*Me,* the leading man . . ." He lifted an elegant two-toned shoe—with a flapping sole—"In these!"

"But by golly you got here." Dad's chubby face was beaming. Then suddenly he broke down—Dad, who never cried. "We're together!"

Together. The best present we could give one another, we realized. All of us. Just being here in the old house where we'd shared so many Christmases. No gift on our lavish lists, if they could materialize, could equal that.

In most Christmases since that memorable one we've been lucky. During the years our children were growing up there were no separations. Then one year, appallingly, history repeated itself. For valid reasons, not a single faraway child could get home. Worse, my husband had flown to Florida for some vital surgery. A proud, brave man—he was adamant about our not coming with him "just because it's Christmas," when he'd be back in another week.

Like my mother before me, I still had one lone chick left—Melanie, fourteen. "We'll get along fine," she said, trying to cheer me.

We built a big fire every evening, went to church, wrapped presents, pretended. But the ache in our hearts kept swelling. And the day before Christmas we burst into mutual tears. "Mommy, it's just not right for Daddy to be down there alone!"

"I know it!" Praying for a miracle, I ran to the telephone. The airlines were hopeless, but there was one roomette available on the last train to Miami. Almost hysterical with relief, we threw things into bags. And what a Christmas Eve! Excited as conspirators, we cuddled together in that cozy space. Melanie hung a tiny wreath in the window and we settled down to watch the endless pageantry flashing by to the rhythmic clicking song of the rails. Little villages and city streets—all dancing with lights and decorations and sparkling Christmas trees. And cars and snowy countrysides and people—all the people. Each one on his or her special pilgrimage of love and celebration this precious night.

At last we drifted off to sleep. But hours later I awoke to a strange stillness. The train had stopped. And, raising the shade, I peered out on a very small town. Silent, deserted, with only a few lights still burning. And under the bare branches, along a lonely street, a figure was walking. A young man in sailor blues, head bent, hunched under the weight of the sea bag on his shoulders. And I thought—*home!* Poor kid, he's almost home. And I wondered if there was someone still up waiting for him; or if anyone knew he was coming at all. My heart cried out to him, for he was suddenly my own son—and my own ghost, and the soul of us all—driven, so immutably driven by this annual call, "Come home!"

Home for Christmas. There must be some deep psychological reason why we turn so instinctively toward home at this special time. Perhaps we are acting out the ancient story of a man and a woman and a coming child, plodding along with their donkey toward their destination. It was necessary for Joseph, the earthly father, to go home to be taxed. Each male had to return to the city of his birth.

Birth. The tremendous miracle of birth shines through every step and syllable of the Bible story. The long, arduous trip across the mountains of Galilee and Judea was also the journey of a life toward birth. Mary was already in labor when they arrived in Bethlehem, so near the time of her delivery that in desperation, since the inn was full, her husband settled for a humble stable.

The child who was born on that first Christmas grew up to be a man. Jesus. He healed many people, taught us many important things. But the message that has left the most lasting impression and given the most hope and comfort is this: that we do have a home to go to, and there will be an ultimate homecoming. A place where we will indeed be reunited with those we love.

Anyway, that's my idea of heaven. A place where Mother is standing in the door, probably bossing Dad the way she used to about the turkey or the tree, and he's enjoying every minute of it. And old friends and neighbors are streaming in and out and the sense of love and joy and celebration will go on forever. A place where every day will be Christmas, with everybody there together. At home.

The Whole World Comes to Bethlehem on Christmas Day

WILMA W. BURTON

The whole world comes to Bethlehem on Christmas Day
To walk the paths the shepherds trod
While heaven's choir sang praise to God,
Where wise men bearing gold and myrrh
Beheld the star that led them there.

The whole world comes to Bethlehem on Christmas Day
To pause before a manger's door
Where lambs bleat low upon the floor,
There to find an infant sleeping
While angels watch are sweetly keeping.

The whole world comes to Bethlehem on Christmas Day,
And though the room is humble, small,
There is a place for one and all
To enter in and worship here
The newborn Saviour they hold dear.

"Christmas is a quest. May each of us follow his star of faith and find the heart's own Bethlehem."

ESTHER BALDWIN YORK

Homeward Bound

VIRGINIA BLANCK MOORE

My heart is homeward bound these days
Because it's Christmastime.
When I see windows gaily decked
And hear the carols chime,
When I meet parcel-laden folks
Returning smiles with smiles,
My heart goes winging straight across
The intervening miles
To home, to family, and to friends
That childhood days made dear,
To hometown streets where passersby
Greet one with welcoming cheer.
Though years go by, and decades, too,
Still I have always found
When Christmastime makes its approach
My heart is homeward bound.

"A home is the sweetest thing on earth on Christmas day."

GRACE NOLL CROWELL

An Empty Purse

SARAH ORNE JEWETT

Little Miss Debby Gaines was counting the days to Christmas; there were only three, and the weather was bright and warm for the time of year. "I've got to step fast to carry out all my plans," she said to herself. "It seems to me as if it were going to be a beautiful Christmas; it won't be like any I've spent lately, either. I shouldn't wonder if it turned out for the best, my losing that money I always call my Christmas money; anyway I'll do the best I can to make up for it."

Miss Debby was sitting by the window sewing as fast as she could, for the light of the short winter day was going, mending a warm old petticoat and humming a psalm-tune. Suddenly she heard a knock at the door; she lived in two upstairs rooms, and could not see the street.

"Come in!" she said cheerfully, and dropped her lapful of work.

"Why, if it isn't Mrs. Rivers!" she exclaimed with much pleasure.

The guest was a large woman, fashionably dressed. You would have thought that a very elegant blue-jay had come to make a late afternoon call upon such a brown chippy-sparrow as Miss Debby Gaines. Miss Debby felt much honored, and brought forward her best rocking chair; and Mrs. Rivers seated herself and began to rock. Her stiff silk gown creaked as if she were a ship at sea.

"What are you doing—something pretty for Christmas?" she asked.

"It may be for Christmas, but it isn't very pretty," answered Miss Debby with a little laugh and shake of the head. "Tell you the truth, I was mending up a nice warm petticoat that I don't have much use for; I thought I'd give it to old Mrs. Bean, at the poorhouse. She's a complaining, cold old creature, an' she's got poor eye-sight and can't sew, and I thought this would make her real comfortable. It's rather more heavy than I need to wear."

"I've been downtown all the afternoon, and it's so tiresome trying to get anything in the stores," complained Mrs. Rivers. "They push you right away from what you want time to look over. I like to consider what I buy. It's a great burden to me trying to get ready for Christmas, and I thought I shouldn't do anything this year on account of my health. I've had large expenses this autumn. I had to buy new carpets and a new outside garment. I do like to see the pretty things in the stores, but they were so full of people and so hot and disagreeable this afternoon.

Miss Debby had picked up her petticoat and was holding it close to the window while she sewed on the button with firm linen stitches.

"I haven't been down the street for two or three days," she said. "You'll excuse me for goin' on with my work; it's most dark, and I'll be done in a moment; then we can sit an' talk."

"It does me good to come and see you once in a while," said Mrs. Rivers plaintively. "I thought I'd stop on my way home. Last year you had so many pretty little things that you'd been making."

"There aren't any at all this year," answered Miss Debby bravely. "It wasn't convenient, so I thought I'd just try having another kind of a merry Christmas."

"Sometimes I wish I had no more responsibilities than you have. My large house is such a care. Mr. Rivers is very particular about everything, and so am I." She gave a great sigh, and creaked louder than before, but Miss Debby did not find the right sort of consolation to offer, and kept silence. "You enjoy having your pretty house," she ventured to say after a few moments; "you wouldn't like to do with as little as some,"—and Mrs. Rivers shook her head in the dusk, and went on rocking.

"Presents aren't nothing unless the heart goes with them," said Miss Debby boldly at last, "and I think we can show good feelin' in other ways than by bestowing little pin-cushions. Anyway, I've got to find those ways for me this year. 'Tis a day when we New England folks can speak right out to each other, and that does us some good. Somethin' gets in the air. I expect now to enjoy this Christmas myself, though I felt dreadful bad last week, sayin' to myself 'twas the first time I couldn't buy Christmas presents. I didn't know how interested I was goin' to get; you see I've made my little plans."

Then they talked about other things, and Mrs. Rivers grew more cheerful and at last went away. She always found Christmas a melancholy season. She did not like the trouble of giving presents then, or at any other time; but she had her good points, as Miss Debby Gaines always bravely insisted.

Early on Christmas morning Miss Debby woke up with a feeling of happy expectation and could hardly wait to make her cup of tea and eat her little breakfast on the corner of the table before she got out her best bonnet and Sunday cloak to begin her Christmas errands. It was cloudy and dark, but the sunlight came at last, pale and radiant, into the little brown room; and Miss Debby's face matched it with a quiet smile and happy look of eagerness.

"Take neither purse nor scrip," she said to herself as she went downstairs into the street. There was nobody else stirring in the house, but she knew that the poorhouse would be open and its early breakfast past by the time she could get there. It was a mile or so out of town. She hugged a large package under her shawl, and shivered a little at the beginning of her walk. There was no snow, but the heavy hoar-frost glistened on the sidewalks, and the air was sharp.

Old Mrs. Bean was coming out of the great kitchen, and when her friend wished her a merry Christmas she shook her head.

"There ain't anybody to make it merry for me," she said.

"I wish you a happy Christmas" said Miss Debby again; "I've come on purpose to be your first caller, an' I'm going to make you the only present I shall give this year. 'Tis somethin' useful, Mis' Bean; a warm petticoat I've fixed up nice, so's you can put it right on and feel the comfort of it."

The old woman's face brightened. "Why, you are real kind," she said eagerly. "It is the one thing I've been wantin'. Oh yes, dear sakes ain't it a beautiful warm one—one o' the real old-fashioned quilted kind. I always used to have 'em when I was better off. Well, that *is* a present!"

"Now I'm goin', because I can come an' set an' talk with you any day, and today I've got Christmas work," and off Miss Debby went to the heart of the town again.

Christmas was on Tuesday that year, and she opened the door of a little house where a tired-looking young woman stood by an ironing-table and looked at her with surprise. "Why, Miss Gaines!" she exclaimed; "where are you going so early?"

"I wish you a happy Christmas!" said Miss Debby. "I've come to spend the mornin' with you. Just through breakfast? No; the little girls are eatin' away yet. Why, you're late!"

"I didn't mean to be," said the young mother; "but I felt so tired this morning, and pretty sad, too, thinking of last year an' all. So I just let the children sleep. Nelly's got cold and was coughing most all night, and I couldn't bear to get up and begin the day. Mother sent for me to come over to spend Christmas, but I couldn't get the courage to start. She said she'd have some little presents ready for the little girls, and now I'm most sorry I disappointed her."

"That's just why I'm here," said Miss Debby gaily, and with double her usual decision. "No, Nelly's not fit to go out, I can see; and you leave her here with me, an' you just get ready and take Susy and go. Your mother'll think everything of it, and I'll see to things here. Ironin'? Why, 'twill do me good. I feel a little chilly, and Nelly and I can have a grand time. Now you go right off and get ready, and catch the quarter-to-nine train. I won't hear no words about it."

So presently the pale, hard-worked young mother put on her widow's bonnet and started off down the street, leading bright-faced little Susy by the hand; and Miss Debby and her favorite, Nelly, watched them go from the window. The breakfast dishes were washed and put away in such fashion that Nelly thought it quite as good as doll's housekeeping; and then, while Miss Debby ironed, she sat in a warm corner by the stove and listened to stories and to Miss Debby's old-fashioned ballads, which, though sung in a slightly cracked voice, were most delightful to childish ears. What a Christmas morning it was! And after the small ironing was done, what pleasant things there seemed to be to do! Miss Debby rummaged until she found some little aprons cut for the children; and first she basted one for Nelly to sew, and then she took the other herself, and they sat down together and sewed until dinner-time. The aprons were pink and added to the gaiety of the occasion; and they were ready at last to surprise Nelly's mother by being put back in their

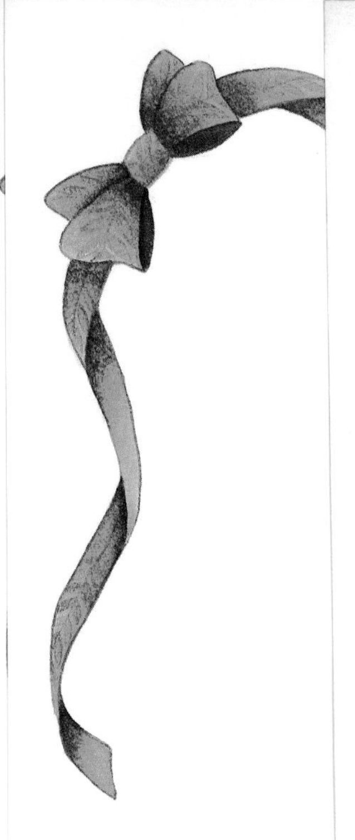

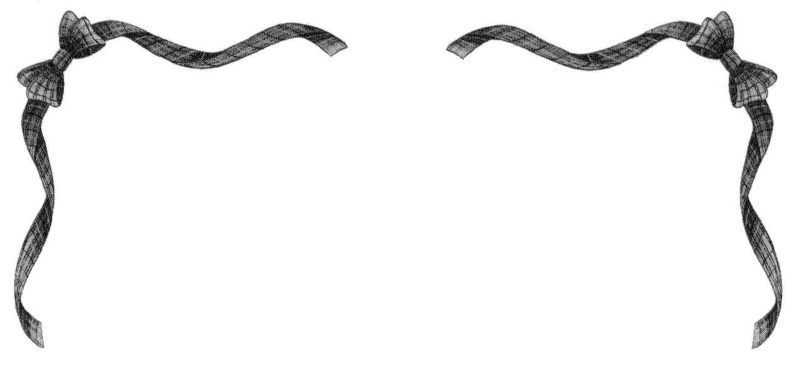

Christmas SENSATIONS

Roasting turkey,

baking pies,

Ice cold air and

starry skies,

Friends and family

warm inside—

This is Christmas!

Wet Your Whistle and Warm Your Toes
Jane Wooster Scott/Superstock

MIKE'S SNACKS
HOT COCOA
SPECIAL
TREATS

Jingle Bells

WORDS AND MUSIC BY J. PIERPONT

Christmas in the Woods

FRANCES FROST

Tonight when the hoar frost falls on the wood,
And the rabbit cowers, and the squirrel is cold,
And the horned owl huddles against a star,
And the drifts are deep, and the year is old,
All shy creatures will think of Him.
The shivering mouse, the hare, the wild young fox,
The doe with the startled fawn
Will dream of gentleness and a Child.

The buck with budding horns will turn
His starry eyes to a silver hill tonight,
The chipmunk will awake and stir
And leave his burrow for the chill, dark midnight,
And all the timid things will pause and sigh, and sighing, bless
That Child who loves the trembling hearts,
The shy hearts of the wilderness.

"Blessed is the season which engages the whole world in a conspiracy of love."

HAMILTON WRIGHT MABIE

San Juan National Forest, Colorado
Jeff Gnass Photography

The Christmas Landscape

WINTER'S AWESOME WONDERS

In memory, the Christmases of my childhood are blessed by a blanket of glistening white snow—snow which meant warm, glowing fires, woolen mittens and sweaters, sleek new sleds, snowmen, snowball fights, sleigh rides and more. I've heard it wistfully wondered aloud more than once by an adult looking out upon a bleak, brown December landscape, remembering the Christmases of their youth; "Where," they want to know, "have the white Christmases gone?"—Emma Golden

A Winter Walk

HENRY DAVID THOREAU

The wind has gently murmured through the blinds, or puffed with feathery softness against the windows, and occasionally sighed like a summer zephyr lifting the leaves along, the live-long night. The meadow mouse has slept in his snug gallery in the sod, the owl has sat in a hollow tree in the depth of the swamp, the rabbit, the squirrel, and the fox have all been housed. The watch-dog has lain quiet on the hearth, and the cattle have stood silent in their stalls. The earth itself has slept, as it were its first, not its last sleep, save when some street sign or woodhouse door has faintly creaked upon its hinge, cheering forlorn nature at her midnight work—the only sound awake 'twixt Venus and Mars—advertising us of a remote inward warmth, a divine cheer and fellowship, where gods are met together, but where it is very bleak for men to stand. But while the earth has slumbered, all the air has been alive with feathery flakes descending, as if some northern Ceres reigned, showering her silvery grain over all the fields.

We sleep, and at length awake to the still reality of a winter morning. The snow lies warm as cotton or down upon the windowsill; the broadened sash and frosted panes admit a dim and private light, which enhances the snug cheer within. The stillness of the morning is impressive. The floor creaks under our feet as we move toward the window to look abroad through some clear space over the fields. We see the roofs stand under their snow burden. From the eaves and fences hang stalactites of snow, and in the yard stand stalagmites covering some concealed core. The trees and shrubs rear white arms to the sky on every side; and where were walls and fences, we see fantastic forms stretching in frolic gambols across the dusky landscape, as if Nature had strewn her fresh designs over the fields by night as models for man's art.

Silently we unlatch the door, letting the drift fall in, and step abroad to face the cutting air. Already the stars have lost some of their sparkle, and a dull, leaden mist skirts the horizon. A lurid brazen light in the east proclaims the approach of day, while the western landscape is dim and spectral still, and clothed in a somber Tartarean light, like the shadowy realms. They are Infernal sounds only that you hear—the crowing of cocks, the barking of dogs, the chopping of wood, the lowing of kine, all seem to come from Pluto's barnyard and beyond the Styx—not for any melancholy they suggest, but their twilight bustle is too solemn and mysterious for earth. The recent tracks of the fox or otter, in the yard, remind us that each hour of the night is crowded with events, and the primeval nature is still working and making tracks in the snow. Opening the gate, we tread briskly along the lone country road, crunching the dry and crisped snow under our feet, or aroused by the sharp, clear creak of the wood sled, just starting for the distant market, from the early farmer's door, where it has lain the summer long, dreaming amid the chips and stubble; while far through the drifts and powdered windows we see the farmer's early candle, like a paled star, emitting a lonely beam, as if some severe virtue were at its matins there. And one by one the smokes begin to ascend from the chimneys amid the trees and snows.

The sluggish smoke curls up
    from some deep dell,
The stiffened air exploring in the dawn,
And making slow acquaintance with the day
Delaying now upon its heavenward course,
In wreathèd loiterings dallying with itself,
With as uncertain purpose and slow deed
As its half-awakened master by the hearth,
Whose mind still slumbering
    and sluggish thoughts
Have not yet swept into the onward current
Of the new day—and now it streams afar,
The while the chopper goes with step direct,
And mind intent to swing the early ax.
First in the dusky dawn he sends abroad

American Winter Scene, a Country Cabin. Currier & Ives/Superstock.

His early scout, his emissary, smoke,
The earliest, latest pilgrim from the roof,
To feel the frosty air, inform the day;
And while he crouches still beside the hearth,
Nor musters courage to unbar the door,
It has gone down the glen with the light wind,
And o'er the plain unfurled its venturous wreath,
Draped the treetops, loitered upon the hill,
And warmed the pinions of the early bird;
And now, perchance, high in the crispy air,
Has caught sight of the day o'er the earth's
edge,
And greets its master's eye at his low door,
As some refulgent cloud in the upper sky.

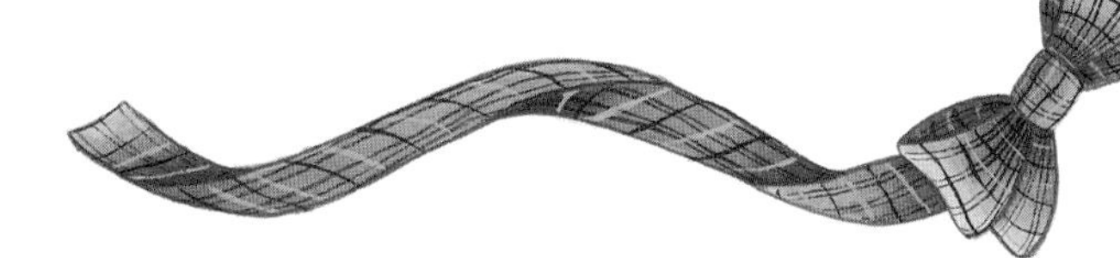

A Christmas Carol

JAMES RUSSELL LOWELL

"What means this glory round our feet,"
The Magi mused, "more bright than morn?"
And voices chanted clear and sweet,
"Today the Prince of Peace is born!"

"What means that star," the Shepherds said,
"That brightens through the rocky glen?"
And angels, answering overhead,
Sang, "Peace on earth, good will to men!"

It's eighteen hundred years and more
Since those sweet oracles were dumb;
We wait for Him, like them of yore;
Alas, He seems so slow to come!

But it was said, in words of gold
No time or sorrow ever shall dim,
That little children might be bold
In perfect trust to come to Him.

All round about our feet shall shine
A light like that the wise men saw,
If we our loving wills incline
To that sweet life which is the law.

So shall we learn to understand
The simple faith of shepherds then,
And, clasping kindly hand in hand,
Sing, "Peace on earth, good will to men!"

And they who do their souls no wrong,
But keep at eve the faith of morn,
Shall daily hear the angel-song,
"Today the Prince of Peace is born!"

Joy in Freetown

EDNA LEWIS

Around Christmastime the kitchens of Freetown, Virginia, would grow fragrant with the baking of cakes, fruit puddings, cookies, and candy. Exchanging gifts was not a custom at that time, but we did look forward to hanging our stockings from the mantel and finding them filled on Christmas morning with tasty "imported" nuts from Lahore's, our favorite hard candies with the cinnamon-flavored red eye, and oranges whose special Christmas aroma reached us at the top of the stairs. And for us four girls, there would also be little celluloid dolls with movable arms and legs that we so loved, and new paper dolls with their fascinating clip-on wardrobes. But mainly getting ready for Christmas meant preparing all kinds of delicious foods that we would enjoy with our families and friends during the days between Christmas Eve and New Year's Day.

There was a special excitement in the kitchens, as many of the things we prepared were foods we tasted only at Christmas. This was the only time in the year when we had oranges, almonds, Brazil nuts, and raisins that came in clusters. And although we were miles from the sea, at Christmas one of the treats we always looked forward to was oysters. The oysters were delivered to Lahore's in barrels on Christmas Eve day, and late on Christmas Eve we would climb the steps over the pasture fence and walk along the path through the woods to the store, carrying our covered tin pails. Mr. Jackson, the storekeeper, would fill some of our pails with oysters. And before we left he always filled our hands with nuts and candy.

We were excited by all the preparations for Christmas, but my own favorite chores were chopping the nuts and raisins for Mother and stirring the wonderful-smelling dark mixtures of fruits . . . that would go into the fruitcake and plum pudding, and decorating the house with evergreens.

Just before Christmas a green lacy vine called running cedar appeared in the woods around Freetown, and we would gather yards and yards of it. We draped everything in the house with it: windows, doors, even the large gilded frames that held the pictures of each of my aunts and uncles. We picked the prickly branches of a giant holly tree—the largest holly I've ever seen—which grew on the top of a nearby hill, and we cut armloads of pine boughs and juniper. My mother always gave the fireplace and hearth a fresh whitewashing the day before Christmas, and washed, starched, and ironed the white lace curtains. On Christmas Eve my father would set up the tree in one corner of the room and we would decorate it with pink, white, and blue strings of popcorn that we had popped, dipped in colored sugar water, and carefully threaded. Small white candles nestled on tufts of cotton were the last decorations to be placed on the tree.

I loved the way the greens looked set off by the white hearth and walls and the stiff white curtains which they draped. In the evenings the soft orange glow from the fire and from the candlelight and the fragrance of the cedar and juniper mingling with the smell of chestnuts roasting always made me wish that Christmas week would last until spring, though I suspected that my mother did not share my wish.

The celebration of Christmas Day began before daybreak with the shooting off of Roman candles. With a great roaring noise they exploded into balls of red fire arcing into the still-dark sky. After they had all been set off, my father would light sparklers for us. We could never imagine Christmas without Roman candles and sparklers; for us it was the most important part of the whole day.

Finally we would go back into the warmth of the house for breakfast. There would be eggs and sausages and plates of hot biscuits with my mother's best preserves, and pan-fried oysters which would taste so sweet, crispy, and delicious.

We all dressed in our Sunday dresses for

Christmas dinner. Dinner was at noon so that we would be finished in time for the men to feed the animals before dark. My mother would have been in the kitchen since five o'clock and half of the night as well, and when the dinner was ready we would gather round the table and sit for hours enjoying all the things she had prepared.

Christmas week was spent visiting back and forth, as at this time of year the men were able to take off some time. The women enjoyed tasting each other's baking and the men took pleasure in comparing the wines they had made at harvest time—wild plum, elderberry, dandelion, and grape. . . .

Every household had a sideboard or a food safe, and these would be laden throughout the week with all the foods that had been made for the holiday. Ours would hold baked ham, smothered rabbit, a pan of mixed small birds that had been trapped in the snow, braised guinea hen, liver pudding, and sometimes a roasted wild turkey that had grown up with our own flock (but usually a fat roast hen), and all the sweet and pungent pickles my mother had made from cucumbers and watermelon rind, crab apples and peaches. The open shelf of the sideboard would be lined with all the traditional holiday cakes: caramel and coconut layer cakes, pound cake, and my mother's rich, dark, flavorful fruitcake. There were plates of fudge and peanut brittle and crocks filled with crisp sugar cookies. The food safe was filled with mince pies, and fruit pies made with the canned fruit of summer.

Although there were no exceptions to our usual custom of sitting down together three times a day for meals, during Christmas week we were free to return to the food safe as many times a day as we liked and my mother would never say a word. But at the end of holiday week we were all given a home-brewed physic which was really vile! It was so vile I've never quite forgotten the taste of it.

On New Year's Day when all the Christmas decorations were taken down, we felt sad and let down; to us our house looked drab and naked, and although the visiting back and forth would continue until winter came to an end, Christmas was over.

***"God grant you the light in Christmas, which is faith;
the warmth of Christmas, which is love;
the radiance of Christmas, which is purity;
the righteousness of Christmas, which is justice;
the belief in Christmas, which is truth;
the all of Christmas, which is Christ ."***

WILDA ENGLISH

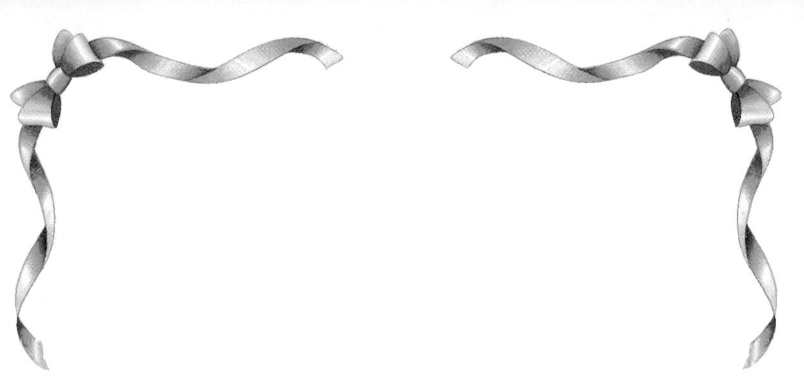

Christmas CELEBRATIONS

Home they come from

far and near,

Those whom family

ties hold dear;

Laughing love and

wholesome cheer,

This is Christmas!

A Happening on Foxboro Pond
Jane Wooster Scott/Superstock

FOXBORO GENERAL STORE
U.S.
POST OFFICE

Go Tell It on the Mountain

SPIRITUAL

P.V. BIANCHI

Christmas Carol

PAUL LAURENCE DUNBAR

Ring out, ye bells!
All Nature swells
With gladness of the wondrous story—
The world was lorn;
But Christ is born
To change our sadness into glory.

Sing, earthlings, sing!
Tonight a King
Hath come from heaven's high throne to bless us.
The outstretched hand
O'er all the land
Is raised in pity to caress us.

Come at His call;
Be joyful all;
Away with mourning and with sadness!
The heavenly choir
With holy fire
Their voices raise in songs of gladness.

The darkness breaks
And Dawn awakes,
Her cheeks suffused with youthful blushes.
The rocks and stones
In holy tones
Are singing sweeter than the thrushes.

Then why should we
In silence be,
When Nature lends her voice to praises;
When heaven and earth
Proclaim the truth
Of Him for whom the lone star blazes?

No, be not still,
But with a will
Strike all your harps and set them ringing;
On hill and heath
Let every breath
Throw all its power into singing!

"The light that shines from the humble manger is strong enough to lighten our way to the end of our days."

AUTHOR UNKNOWN

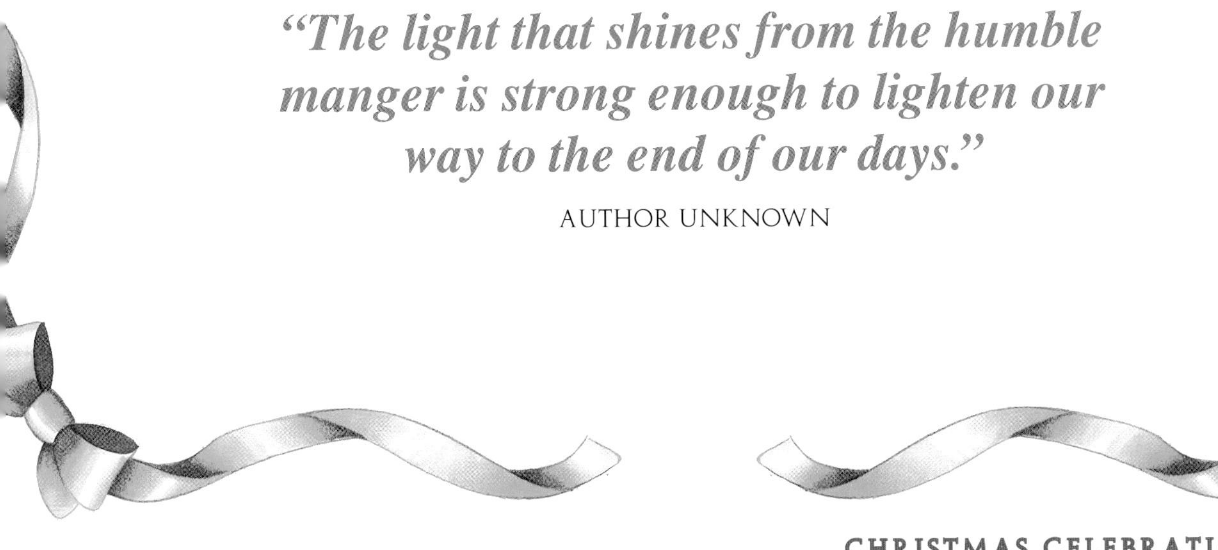

A Day of Pleasant Bread

DAVID GRAYSON

They have all gone now, and the house is very still. For the first time this evening I can hear the familiar sound of the December wind blustering about the house, complaining at closed doorways, asking questions at the shutters; but here in my room, under the green reading lamp, it is warm and still. Although Harriet has closed the doors, covered the coals in the fireplace, and said good night, the atmosphere still seems to tingle with the electricity of genial humanity.

The parting voice of the Scotch Preacher still booms in my ears:

"This," said he, as he was going out of our door, wrapped like an Arctic highlander in cloaks and tippets, "has been a day of pleasant bread."

One of the very pleasantest I can remember!

I sometimes think we expect too much of Christmas Day. We try to crowd into it the long arrears of kindliness and humanity of the whole year. As for me, I like to take my Christmas a little at a time, all through the year. And thus I drift along into the holidays—let them overtake me unexpectedly—waking up some fine morning and suddenly saying to myself, "Why, this is Christmas Day!"

How the discovery makes one bound out of his bed! What a new sense of life and adventure it imparts! Almost anything may happen on a day like this—one thinks. I may meet friends I have not seen before in years. Who knows? I may discover that this is a far better and kindlier world than I had ever dreamed it could be.

So I sing out to Harriet as I go down, "Merry Christmas, Harriet"—and not waiting for her sleepy reply I go down and build the biggest, warmest, friendliest fire of the year. Then I get into my thick coat and mittens and open the back door. All around the sill, deep on the step, and all about the yard lies the drifted snow: It has transformed my wood pile into a grotesque Indian mound, and it frosts the roof of my barn like a wedding cake. I go at it lustily with my wooden shovel, clearing out a pathway to the gate.

Cold, too; one of the coldest mornings we've had—but clear and very still. The sun is just coming up over the hill near Horace's farm. From Horace's chimney the white woodsmoke of an early fire rises straight upward, all golden with sunshine, into the measureless blue of the sky—on its way to heaven, for aught I know. When I reach the gate my blood is racing warmly in my veins. I straighten my back, thrust my shovel into the snow pile, and shout at the top of my voice, for I can no longer contain myself:

"Merry Christmas, Harriet."

Harriet opens the door—just a crack.

"Merry Christmas yourself, you Arctic explorer! Oo—but it's cold!"

And she closes the door.

Upon hearing these riotous sounds the barnyard suddenly awakens. I hear my horse whinnying from the barn, the chickens begin to crow and cackle, and such a grunting and squealing as the pigs set up from behind the straw stack, it would do a man's heart good to hear!

"It's a friendly world," I say to myself, "and full of business."

I plow through the snow to the stable door. I scuff and stamp the snow away and pull it open with difficulty. A cloud of steam arises out of the warmth within. I step inside. My horse raises his head above the stanchion, looks around at me, and strikes his forefoot on the stable floor—the best greeting he has at his command for a fine Christmas morning. My cow, until now silent, begins to bawl.

I lay my hand on the horse's flank and he steps over in his stall to let me go by. I slap his neck and he lays back his ears playfully. Thus I go out into the passageway and give my horse his oats, throw corn and stalks to the pigs and a handful of grain to Harriet's chickens (it's the only way to stop the cackling!). And thus presently the barnyard is quiet again except for the sound of contented feeding.

Take my word for it, this is one of the pleasant moments of life. I stand and look long at my barnyard family. I observe with satisfaction how plump they are and how well they are bearing the winter. Then I look up at my mountainous straw stack with its capping of snow, and my corn crib with the yellow ears visible through the slats, and my barn with its mow full of hay—all the gatherings of the year, now being expended in growth. I cannot at all explain it, but at such moments the circuit of that dim spiritual battery which each of us conceals within seems to close, and the full current of contentment flows through our lives.

All the morning as I went about my chores I had a peculiar sense of expected pleasure. It seemed certain to me that something unusual and adventurous was about to happen—and if it did not happen offhand, why I was there to make it happen! When I went in to breakfast (do you know the fragrance of broiling bacon when you have worked for an hour before breakfast on a morning of zero weather? If you do not, consider that heaven still has gifts in store for you!)—when I went into breakfast, I fancied that Harriet looked preoccupied, but I was too busy just then (hot corn muffins) to make an inquiry, and I knew by experience that the best solvent of secrecy is patience.

"David," said Harriet, presently, "the cousins can't come!"

"Can't come!" I exclaimed.

"Why, you act as if you were delighted."

"No—well, yes," I said, "I knew that some extraordinary adventure was about to happen!"

"Adventure! It's a cruel disappointment—I was all ready for them."

"Harriet," I said, "adventure is just what we make it. And aren't we to have the Scotch Preacher and his wife?"

"But I've got such a good dinner."

"Well," I said, "there are no two ways about it: it must be eaten. You may depend upon me to do my duty."

"We'll have to send out into the highways and compel them to come in," said Harriet ruefully.

I had several choice observations I should have liked to make upon this problem, but Harriet was plainly not listening; she sat with her eyes fixed reflectively on the coffeepot. I watched her for a moment, then I remarked, "There aren't any."

"David," she exclaimed, "how did you know what I was thinking about?"

"I merely wanted to show you," I said, "that my genius is not properly appreciated in my own household. You thought of highways, didn't you? Then you thought of the poor; especially the poor on Christmas Day; then of Mrs. Heney, who isn't poor anymore, having married John Daniels; and then I said, 'There aren't any.'"

Harriet laughed.

"It has come to a pretty pass," she said, "when there are no poor people to invite to dinner on Christmas Day."

"It's a tragedy, I'll admit," I said, "but let's be logical about it."

"I am willing," said Harriet, "to be as logical as you like."

"Then," I said, "having no poor to invite to dinner we must necessarily try the rich. That's logical, isn't it?"

"Who?" asked Harriet, which is just like a woman. Whenever you get a good healthy argument started with her, she will suddenly shortcircuit it, and want to know if you mean Mr. Smith, or Joe Perkins's boys, which I maintain is not logical.

"Well, there are the Starkweathers," I said.

"David!"

"They're rich, aren't they?"

"Yes, but you know how they live—what dinners they have; and besides, they probably have a houseful of company."

"Weren't you telling me the other day how many people who were really suffering were too proud to let anyone know about it? Weren't you advising the necessity of getting acquainted with people and finding out—tactfully, of course you made a point of tact—what the trouble was?"

"But I was talking of poor people."

"Why shouldn't a rule that is good for poor people be equally good for rich people? Aren't they proud?"

"Oh, you can argue,'" observed Harriet.

"And I can act, too," I said. "I am now going over to invite the Starkweathers. I heard a rumor that their cook has left them and I expect to find them starving in their parlor. Of course they'll be very haughty and proud, but I'll be tactful, and when I go away I'll casually leave a diamond tiara in the front hall."

"What is the matter with you this morning?"

"Christmas," I said.

I can't tell how pleased I was with the enterprise I had in mind; it suggested all sorts of amusing and surprising developments. Moreover, I left Har-

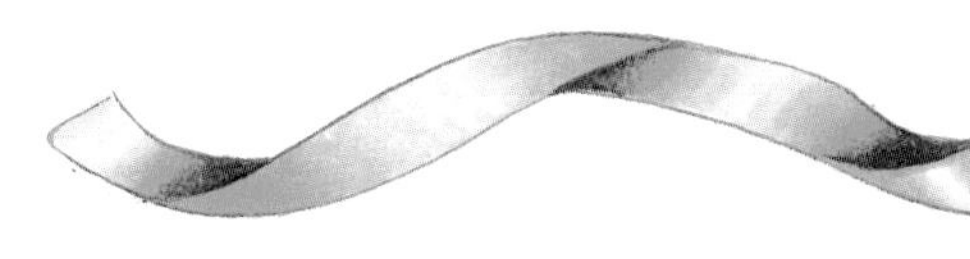

riet, finally, in the breeziest of spirits, having quite forgotten her disappointment over the non-arrival of the cousins.

"If you should get the Starkweathers . . ."

"In the bright lexicon of youth," I observed, "there is no such word as fail."

So I set off up the town road . . . snow everywhere—the fences half-hidden, the bridges clogged, the trees laden: where the road was hard it squeaked under my feet, and where it was soft I strode through the drifts. And the air went to one's head like wine! . . . And I thought how happy everyone must be on a Christmas morning like this! At the hill bridge who should I meet but the Scotch preacher himself, God bless him!

"Well, well, David," he exclaimed heartily, "Merry Christmas.

I drew my face down and said solemnly:

"Dr. McAlway, I am on a most serious errand."

"Why, now, what's the matter?" He was all sympathy at once.

"I am out in the highways trying to compel the poor of this neighborhood to come to our feast."

The Scotch Preacher observed me with a twinkle in his eye.

"David," he said, putting his hand to his mouth as if to speak in my ear, "here is a poor man you will na' have to compel."

"Oh, you don't count," I said. "You're coming anyhow."

Then I told him of the errand with our millionaire friends, into the spirit of which he entered with the greatest zest. He was full of advice and much excited lest I fail to do a thoroughly competent job. For a moment I think he wanted to take the whole thing out of my hands.

"Man, man, it's a lovely thing to do," he exclaimed, "but I ha' me doots—I ha' me doots." . . .

So I left him and went onward toward the Starkweathers'. Presently I saw the great house standing among its wintry trees. There was smoke in the chimney but no other evidence of life. At the gate my spirits, which had been of the best all the morning, began to fail me. Though Harriet and I were well enough acquainted with the Starkweathers, yet at this late moment on Christmas morning it did seem rather a hairbrained scheme to think of inviting them to dinner. . . .

I waited in the reception-room, which was cold and felt damp. In the parlor beyond I could see the innumerable things of beauty—furniture, pictures, books, so very, very much of everything—with which the room was filled. I saw it now, as I had often seen it before, with a peculiar sense of weariness. How all these things, though beautiful enough in themselves, must clutter up a man's life! . . .

Presently Mr. Starkweather appeared in the doorway. He wore a velvet smoking-jacket and slippers; and somehow, for a bright morning like this, he seemed old, and worn, and cold.

"Well, well, friend," he said, "I'm glad to see you."

He said it as though he meant it.

"Come into the library; it's the only room in the whole house that is comfortably warm. You've no idea what a task it is to heat a place like this in really cold weather. No sooner do I find a man who can run my furnace than he goes off and leaves me.

"I can sympathize with you," I said, "we often have trouble at our house with the man who builds the fires."

He looked around at me quizzically.

"He lies too long in bed in the morning," I said.

By this time we had arrived at the library, where a bright fire was burning in the grate. It was a fine big room, with dark oak furnishings and books in cases along one wall, but this morning it had a disheveled and untidy look. On a little table at one side of the fireplace were the remains of a breakfast; at the other a number of wraps were thrown carelessly upon a chair. As I came in Mrs. Starkweather rose from her place, drawing a silk scarf round her shoulders. She is a robust, rather handsome woman with many rings on her fingers, and a pair of glasses hanging to a little gold hook on her ample bosom; but this morning she, too, looked worried and old.

"Oh, yes," she said with a rueful laugh, "we're beginning a merry Christmas, as you see. Think of Christmas with no cook in the house!"

I felt as if I had discovered a gold mine. Poor starving millionaires.

But Mrs. Starkweather had not told the whole of her sorrowful story.

"We had a company of friends invited for dinner today," she said, and our cook was ill—or said she was—and had to go. One of the maids went with her. The man who looks after the furnace disappeared on Friday. . . . We can't very well leave the place without someone who is responsible in charge of it—and so here we are. Merry Christmas!"

I couldn't help laughing. Poor people!

"You might," I said, "apply for Mrs. Heney's place."

"Who is Mrs. Heney?" asked Mrs. Starkweather.

"You don't mean to say that you never heard of Mrs. Heney!" I exclaimed. "Mrs. Heney, who is now Mrs. 'Penny' Daniels? You've missed one of our greatest celebrities."

With that, of course, I had to tell them about Mrs. Heney, who has for years performed a most important function in this community. Alone and unaided she has been the poor whom we are supposed to have always with us. If it had not been for the devoted faithfulness of Mrs. Heney at Thanksgiving, Christmas, and other times of the year, I suppose our Woman's Aid Society and the King's Daughters would have perished miserably of undistributed turkeys and tufted comforters. For years Mrs. Heney filled the place most acceptably. Curbing the natural outpourings of a rather jovial soul she could upon occasion look as deserving of charity as any person that ever I met. But I pitied the little Heneys: it always comes hard on the children. For weeks after every Thanksgiving and Christmas they always wore a painfully stuffed and suffocated look. I only came to appreciate fully what a self-sacrificing public servant Mrs. Heney really was when I learned that she had taken the desperate alternative of marrying "Penny" Daniels.

"So you think we might possibly aspire to the position?" laughed Mrs. Starkweather.

Upon this I told them of the trouble in our household and asked them to come down and help us enjoy Dr. McAlway and the goose. When I left, after much more pleasant talk, they both came with me to the door seeming greatly improved in spirits.

"You've given us something to live for, Mr. Grayson," said Mrs. Starkweather.

So I walked homeward in the highest spirits, and an hour or more later who should we see in the top of our upper field but Mr. Starkweather and his wife floundering in the snow. They reached the lane literally covered from top to toe with snow and both of them ruddy with cold.

"We walked over," said Mrs. Starkweather breathlessly, "and I haven't had so much fun in years." . . .

I can't pretend to describe Harriet's dinner: the gorgeous brown goose, and the applesauce, and all the other things that best go with it, and the pumpkin pie at the end—the finest, thickest, most delicious pumpkin pie I ever ate in all my life. It melted in one's mouth and brought visions of celestial bliss. And I wish I could have a picture of Harriet presiding. I have never seen her happier, or more in her element. Every time she brought in a new dish or took off a cover it was a sort of miracle. And her coffee—But I must not and dare not elaborate. And what great talk we had afterward.

I've known the Scotch Preacher for a long time, but I never saw him in quite such a mood of hilarity. He and Mr. Starkweather told stories of their boyhood—and we laughed, and laughed—Mrs. Starkweather the most of all. Seeing her so often in her carriage, or in the dignity of her home, I didn't think she had so much jollity in her. Finally she discovered Harriet's cabinet organ and nothing would do but she must sing for one.

"None of the newfangled ones, Clara," cried her husband: "Some of the old ones we used to know." So she sat herself down at the organ and threw her head back and began to sing. . . . Mr. Starkweather jumped up and ran over to the organ and joined in with his deep voice. Harriet and I followed. The Scotch Preacher's wife nodded in time with the music, and presently I saw the tears in her eyes. As for Dr. McAlway, he sat on the edge of his chair with his hands on his knees and wagged his shaggy head, and before we got through he, too, joined in with his big sonorous voice. . . .

Oh, I can't tell here—it grows late and there's work tomorrow—all the things we did and said. They stayed until it was dark, and when Mrs. Starkweather was ready to go, she took both of Harriet's hands in hers and said with great earnestness:

"I haven't had such a good time at Christmas since I was a little girl. I shall never forget it."

And the dear old Scotch Preacher, when Harriet and I had wrapped him up, went out, saying:

"This has been a day of pleasant bread." . . .

It has; it has. I shall not soon forget it. . . .

It's Christmastime

HARRIET FELTHAM

It's Christmastime, it's Christmastime,
The church bells say in every chime,
A time for work and care to cease;
Give praises to the Prince of Peace.

It's Christmastime, it's Christmastime,
A day for joy in every clime,
To celebrate the Christ Child's birth
And foster peace upon this earth.

Fir trees will shine with glowing light
To cheer a stranger through the night
And take a hand in brotherhood
For faith, for love and all that's good.

Carols will ring through cold, crisp air
While families gather everywhere;
And up above the stars will shine
Much brighter, for it's Christmastime!

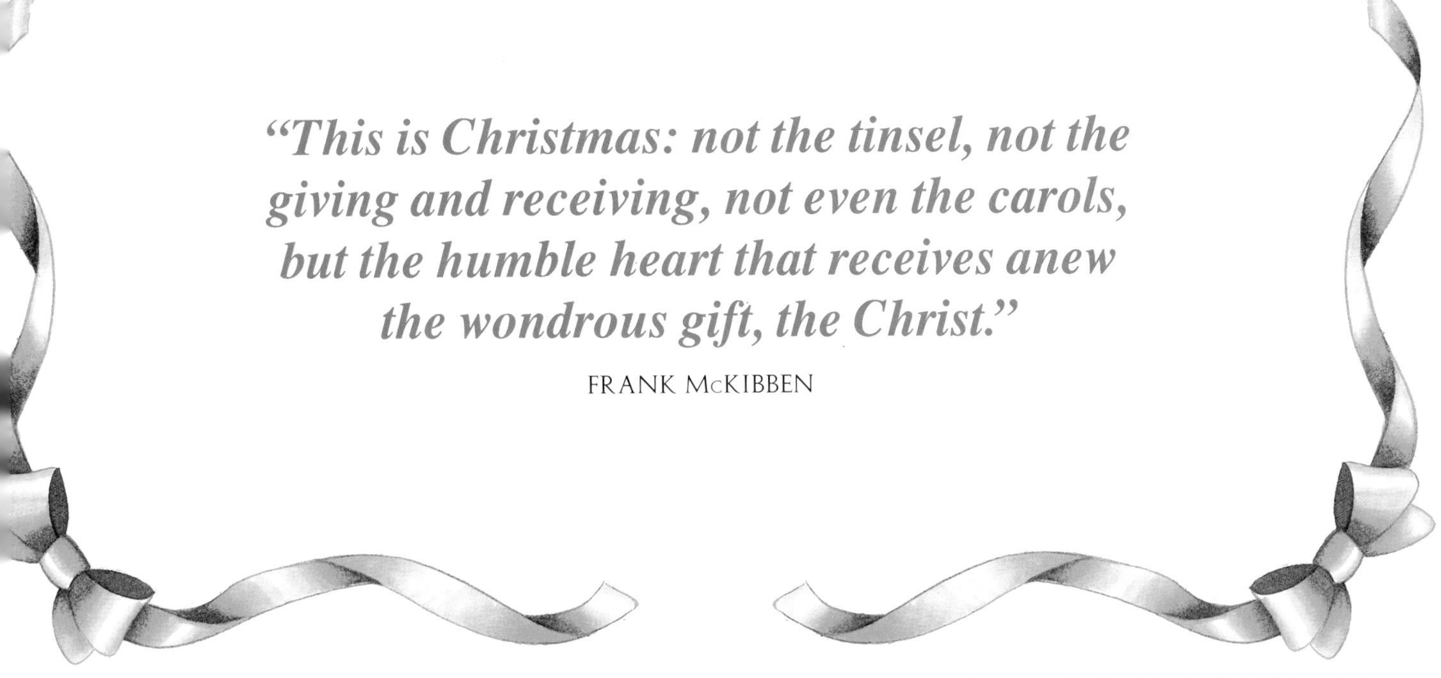

"This is Christmas: not the tinsel, not the giving and receiving, not even the carols, but the humble heart that receives anew the wondrous gift, the Christ."

FRANK McKIBBEN

Santa Claus

AN AMERICAN TRADITION

The Santa Claus I remember from childhood is the one on the cover of the old Harper's *magazines that my grandmother pulled out each December for us children to look at. He was rosy cheeked and plump as could be, with the bright red suit and snow-white beard we see everywhere at Christmastime nowadays. He lived at the North Pole and cared for his reindeer and kept close tabs on the behavior of all boys and girls. Gramma told us that the man who drew these Santas was named Thomas Nast, and that although he spent most of the year drawing political cartoons, each Christmas he thought back to his boyhood in Bavaria and to the warm-hearted elf named Santa Claus—St. Nicholas—that the Bavarian children had loved. For me, and for generations of American children, Thomas Nast's Santa became the one and only Santa, the one who made our childhood dreams come true.—Stephen Ott*

"Caught!" by Thomas Nast. From *Harper's Weekly,* December 24, 1881.

"Merry Old Santa Claus" by Thomas Nast. From *Harper's Weekly,* January 1, 1881.

"Merry Christmas" by Thomas Nast. From *Harper's Weekly,* January 4, 1879.

"'Hello, Santa Claus!' 'Hello, Little One!'" by Thomas Nast. From *Harper's Weekly,* December 20, 1884.

ıce to Test Santa Claus's Generosity" by Thomas
. From *Harper's Weekly,* December 30, 1876.

"The Coming of Santa Claus" by Thomas Nast, 1872.

"Santa Claus's Mail" by Thomas Nast. From *Harper's Weekly,* December 30, 1871.

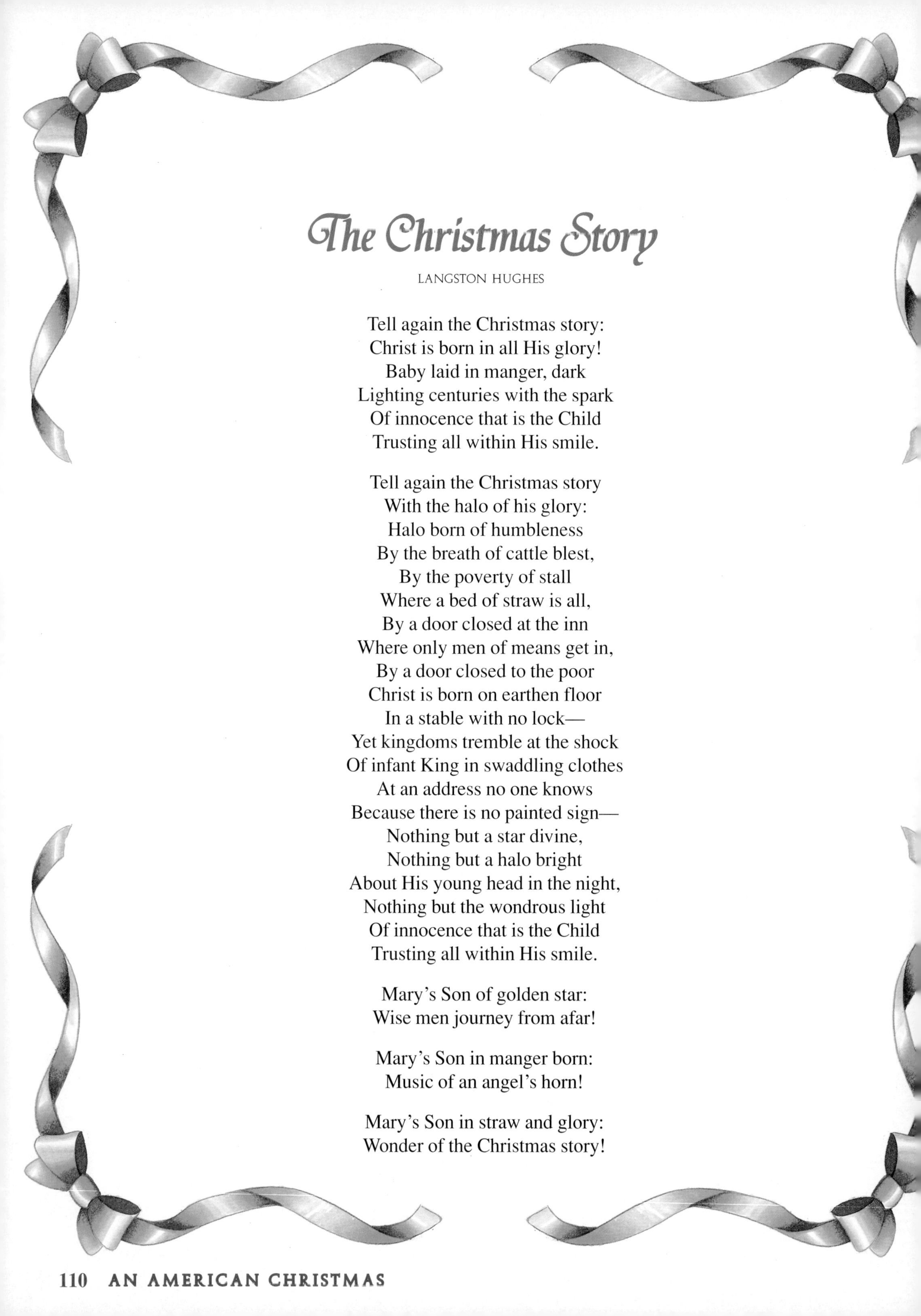

The Christmas Story

LANGSTON HUGHES

Tell again the Christmas story:
Christ is born in all His glory!
Baby laid in manger, dark
Lighting centuries with the spark
Of innocence that is the Child
Trusting all within His smile.

Tell again the Christmas story
With the halo of his glory:
Halo born of humbleness
By the breath of cattle blest,
By the poverty of stall
Where a bed of straw is all,
By a door closed at the inn
Where only men of means get in,
By a door closed to the poor
Christ is born on earthen floor
In a stable with no lock—
Yet kingdoms tremble at the shock
Of infant King in swaddling clothes
At an address no one knows
Because there is no painted sign—
Nothing but a star divine,
Nothing but a halo bright
About His young head in the night,
Nothing but the wondrous light
Of innocence that is the Child
Trusting all within His smile.

Mary's Son of golden star:
Wise men journey from afar!

Mary's Son in manger born:
Music of an angel's horn!

Mary's Son in straw and glory:
Wonder of the Christmas story!

FROM *My Ántonia*

WILLA CATHER

During the week before Christmas, Jake was the most important person of our household, for he was to go to town and do all our Christmas shopping. But on the 21st of December, the snow began to fall. The flakes came down so thickly that from the sitting-room windows I could not see beyond the windmill—its frame looked dim and gray, unsubstantial like a shadow. The snow did not stop falling all day, or during the night that followed. The cold was not severe, but the storm was quiet and resistless. The men could not go farther than the barns and corral. They sat about the house most of the day as if it were Sunday; greasing their boots, mending their suspenders, plaiting whiplashes.

On the morning of the 22d, Grandfather announced at breakfast that it would be impossible to go to Black Hawk for Christmas purchases. Jake was sure he could get through on horseback and bring home our things in saddle-bags; but Grandfather told him the roads would be obliterated. . . .

We decided to have a country Christmas, without any help from town. I had wanted to get some picture books for Yulka and Ántonia; even Yulka was able to read a little now. Grandmother took me into the ice-cold storeroom, where she had some bolts of gingham and sheeting. She cut squares of cotton cloth and we sewed them together into a book. We bound it between pasteboards, which I covered with brilliant calico, representing scenes from a circus. For two days I sat at the dining-room table, pasting this book full of pictures for Yulka. We had files of those good old family magazines which used to publish colored lithographs of popular paintings, and I was allowed to use some of these. I took "Napoleon Announcing the Divorce to Josephine" for my frontispiece. On the white pages I grouped Sunday-school cards and advertising cards which I had brought from my "old country." Fuchs got out the old candle-moulds and made tallow candles. Grandmother hunted up her fancy cake-cutters and baked gingerbread men and roosters, which we decorated with burnt sugar and red cinnamon drops.

On the day before Christmas, Jake packed the things we were sending to the Shimerdas in his saddle-bags and set off on Grandfather's gray gelding. When he mounted his horse at the door, I saw that he had a hatchet slung to his belt, and he gave Grandmother a meaning look which told me he was planning a surprise for me. That afternoon I watched long and eagerly from the sitting-room window. At last I saw a dark spot moving on the west hill, beside the half-buried cornfield, where the sky was taking on a coppery flush from the sun that did not quite break through. I put on my cap and ran out to meet Jake. When I got to the pond I could see that he was bringing in a little cedar tree across his pommel. He used to help my father cut Christmas trees for me in Virginia, and he had not forgotten how much I liked them.

By the time we had placed the cold, fresh-smelling little tree in a corner of the sitting-room, it was already Christmas Eve. After supper we all gathered there, and even Grandfather, reading his paper by the table, looked up with friendly interest now and then. The cedar was about five feet high and very shapely. We hung it with the gingerbread animals, strings of popcorn, and bits of candle which Fuchs had fitted into pasteboard sockets. Its real splendors, however, came from the most unlikely place in the world—from Otto's cowboy trunk. I had never seen anything in that trunk but old boots and spurs and pistols, and a fascinating mixture of yellow leather thongs, cartridges, and shoemaker's wax. From under the lining he now produced a collection of brilliantly colored paper figures, several inches high and stiff enough to stand alone. They had been sent to him year after year, by his old mother in Austria. There was a bleeding heart, in tufts of paper lace; there were the three kings, gorgeously appareled, and the ox and the ass and the shepherds; there was the Baby in the manger, and a group of angels, singing; there were camels and leopards, held by the black slaves of the three kings. Our tree became the talking tree of the fairy tale; legends and stories nestled like birds in its branches. Grandmother said it reminded her of the

Tree of Knowledge. We put sheets of cotton wool under it for a snow field, and Jake's pocket mirror for a frozen lake. . . .

On Christmas morning, when I got down to the kitchen, the men were just coming in from their morning chores—the horses and pigs always had their breakfast before we did. Jake and Otto shouted "Merry Christmas!" to me, and winked at each other when they saw the waffle-irons on the stove. Grandfather came down, wearing a white shirt and his Sunday coat. Morning prayers were longer than usual. He read the chapters from St. Matthew about the birth of Christ, and as we listened it all seemed like something that had happened lately, and near at hand. In his prayer he thanked the Lord for the first Christmas, and for all that it had meant to the world ever since. He gave thanks for our food and comfort, and prayed for the poor and destitute in great cities, where the struggle for life was harder than it was here with us. Grandfather's prayers were often very interesting. He had the gift of simple and moving expression. Because he talked so little, his words had a peculiar force; they were not worn dull from constant use. His prayers reflected what he was thinking about at the time, and it was chiefly through them that we got to know his feelings and his views about things.

After we sat down to our waffles and sausage, Jake told us how pleased the Shimerdas had been with their presents; even Ambrosch was friendly and went to the creek with him to cut the Christmas tree. It was a soft gray day outside, with heavy clouds working across the sky, and occasional squalls of snow. There were always odd jobs to be done about the barn on holidays, and the men were busy until afternoon. Then Jake and I played dominoes, while Otto wrote a long letter home to his mother. He always wrote to her on Christmas Day, he said, no matter where he was, and no matter how long it had been since his last letter. All afternoon he sat in the dining room. He would write for a while, then sit idle, his clenched fist lying on the table, his eyes following the pattern of the oilcloth. He spoke and wrote his own language so seldom that it came to him awkwardly. His effort to remember entirely absorbed him.

At about four o'clock a visitor appeared: Mr. Shimerda, wearing his rabbit-skin cap and collar, and new mittens his wife had knitted. He had come to thank us for the presents, and for all Grandmother's kindness to his family. Jake and Otto joined us from the basement and we sat about the stove, enjoying the deepening gray of the winter afternoon and the atmosphere of comfort and security in my grandfather's house. This feeling seemed completely to take possession of Mr. Shimerda. . . . He sat still and passive, his head resting against the back of the wooden rocking chair, his hands relaxed upon the arms. His face had a look of weariness and pleasure, like that of sick people when they feel relief from pain. . . . He said almost nothing, and smiled rarely; but as he rested there we all had a sense of his utter content.

As it grew dark, I asked whether I might light the Christmas tree before the lamp was brought. When the candle ends sent up their conical yellow flames, all the colored figures from Austria stood out clear and full of meaning against the green boughs. Mr. Shimerda rose, crossed himself, and quietly knelt down before the tree, his head sunk forward. His long body formed a letter "S." I saw Grandmother look apprehensively at Grandfather. He was rather narrow in religious matters, and sometimes spoke out and hurt people's feelings. There had been nothing strange about the tree before, but now, with some one kneeling before it—images, candles—Grandfather merely put his fingertips to his brow and bowed his venerable head. . . .

We persuaded our guest to stay for supper with us. He needed little urging. As we sat down to the table, it occurred to me that he liked to look at us, and that our faces were open books to him. When his deep-seeing eyes rested on me, I felt as if he were looking far ahead into the future for me, down the road I would have to travel.

At nine o'clock Mr. Shimerda lighted one of our lanterns and put on his overcoat and fur collar. He stood in the little entry hall, the lantern and his fur cap under his arm, shaking hands with us. When he took Grandmother's hand, he bent over it as he always did, and said slowly, "Good wo-man!" He made the sign of the cross over me, put on his cap and went off in the dark. As we turned back to the sitting-room, Grandfather looked at me searchingly. "The prayers of all good people are good," he said quietly.

The Christmas Long Ago

JAMES WHITCOMB RILEY

Come, sing a hale Heigh-ho
For the Christmas long ago!
When the old log-cabin homed us
From the night of blinding snow,
When the rarest joy held reign,
And the chimney roared amain,
With the firelight like a beacon
Through the frosty windowpane.

Ah! the revel and the din
From without and from within,
The blend of distant sleigh bells
With the plinking violin;
The muffled shrieks and cries—
Then the glowing cheeks and eyes—
The driving storm of greetings,
Gusts of kisses and surprise.

The eyes that smile alone
Back into our happy own—
The leaping pulse—the laughing blood—
The trembling undertone!—
Ho! pair us off once more,
With our feet upon the floor
And our heads and hearts in heaven,
As they were in days of yore!

Winter in the Country. A Cold Morning.
Currier and Ives/Superstock

The Toy-Strewn Home

EDGAR A. GUEST

Give me the home where the toys are strewn,
Where the dolls are asleep in the chairs,
Where the building blocks and the toy balloon
And the soldiers guard the stairs.
Let me step in a house where the tiny cart
With the horses rules the floor
And rest comes into my weary heart,
For I am at home once more.

Give me the home with the toys about,
With the battered old train of cars,
The box of paints and the books left out,
And the ship with her broken spars.
Let me step in a house at the close of day
That is littered with children's toys,
And dwell once more in the haunts of play,
With the echoes of bygone noise.

Give me the home where the toys are seen,
The house where the children romp;
And I'll happier be than man has been
Neath the gilded dome of pomp.
Let me see the litter of bright-eyed play
Strewn over the parlor floor,
And the joys I knew in a far-off day
Will gladden my heart once more.

Whoever has lived in a toy-strewn home,
Though feeble he be and gray,
Will yearn, no matter how far he roam,
For the glorious disarray
Of the little home with its littered floor
That was his in the bygone days;
And his heart will throb as it throbbed before
When he rests where a baby plays.

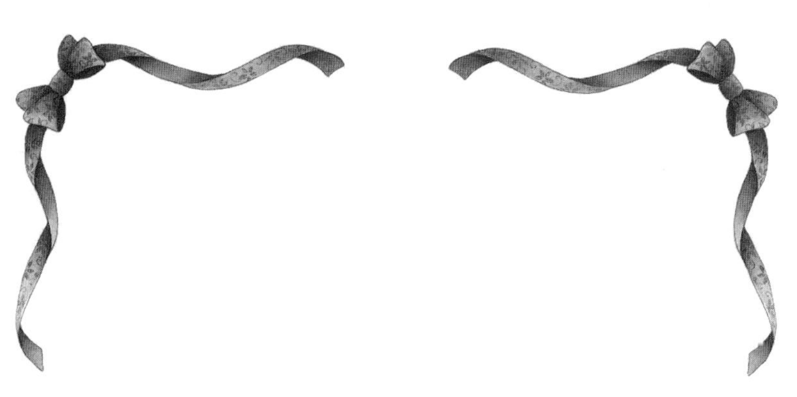

Christmas REFLECTIONS

Memories of days

gone by,

Children's laughter,

family ties,

Old, dear friends and

warm hearth fires—

This is Christmas!

Four-Horse Hitch
Linda Nelson Stocks

I'll Be Home for Christmas

WORDS BY KIM GANNON, MUSIC BY WALTER KENT

The Biltmore Estate
Asheville, North Carolina

A Boy at Christmas

EDGAR A. GUEST

If I could have my wish tonight
It would not be for wealth or fame,
It would not be for some delight
That men who live in luxury claim,
But it would be that I might rise
At three or four A.M. to see
With eager, happy, boyish eyes
My presents on the Christmas tree.
Throughout this world there is no joy,
I know now I am growing gray,
So rich as being just a boy,
A little boy on Christmas Day.

I'd like once more to stand and gaze
Enraptured on a tinseled tree,
With eyes that know just how to blaze,
A heart still tuned to ecstasy;
I'd like to feel the old delight,
The surging thrills within me come;
To love a thing with all my might,
To grasp the pleasure of the drum;
To know the meaning of a toy—
A meaning lost to minds blasé;
To be just once again a boy,
A little boy on Christmas Day.

I'd like to see a pair of skates
The way they looked to me back then,
Before I'd turned from boyhood's gates
And marched into the world of men;
I'd like to see a jackknife, too,
With those same eager, dancing eyes
That couldn't fault or blemish view;
I'd like to feel the same surprise,
The pleasure, free from all alloy,
That has forever passed away,
When I was just a little boy
And had my faith in Christmas Day.

Oh, little laughing roguish lad,
The king that rules across the sea
Would give his scepter if he had
Such joy as now belongs to thee!
And beards of gray would give their gold,
And all the honors they possess,
Once more within their grasp to hold
Thy present fee of happiness.
Earth sends no greater, surer joy,
As, too soon, thou, as I, shall say,
Than that of him who is a boy,
A little boy on Christmas Day.

The Christmas Gift for Mother

EDGAR A. GUEST

In the Christmastimes of the long ago,
There was one event we used to know
That was better than any other;
It wasn't the toys that we hoped to get,
But the talks we had—and I hear them yet—
Of the gift we'd buy for Mother.

If ever love fashioned a Christmas gift,
Or saved its money or practiced thrift.
'Twas done in those days, my brother—
Those golden times of long gone by,
Of our happiest years, when you and I
Talked over the gift for Mother.

We hadn't gone forth on our different ways
Nor coined our lives into yesterdays
In the fires that smelt and smother,
And we whispered and planned in our youthful glee
Of that marvelous "something" which was to be
The gift of our hearts to Mother.

It had to be all that our purse could give,
Something she'd treasure while she could live,
And better than any other.
We gave it the best of our love and thought,
And, Oh, the joy when at last we'd bought
That marvelous gift for Mother!

Now I think as we go on our different ways,
Of the joy of those vanished yesterdays.
How good it would be, my brother,
If this Christmastime we could only know
That same sweet thrill of long ago
When we shared in the gift for Mother.

Christmas Memory Lane
by Erwin L. Hess
CHRISTMAS IS A TIME OF THE YEAR WHEN WE THINK OF OUR OLD, CHILDHOOD NEIGHBORHOOD, OUR OWN LITTLE WORLD OF THE PAST... NOW JUST A MEMORY. THE FEEL OF NEW SNOW AT CHRISTMASTIME TAKES US BACK TO A SPARKLING NIGHT OF YESTERYEAR ....
.... WHEN THE SNOW SQUEAKED AND MEWED BENEATH OUR FEET AS WE TRUDGED ALONG THE ROAD WHERE SLEIGHS, BOBSLEDS AND CUTTERS HAD MADE WALKING EASIER. AS OUR MERRY THOUGHTS CONTINUE TO DRIFT FURTHER BACK TO CHRISTMAS OF YESTERYEAR, A CONGLOMERATION OF OTHER MEMORIES PULLS US BACK INTO THE PAST. EASILY AND SWIFTLY WE FIND OURSELVES NO LONGER TRUDGING, BUT SCAMPERING DOWN.....
Memory Lane!
AND, ...
ONCE WE ARE ON MEMORY LANE, IT'S EASY FOR US TO POKE THROUGH THE HAZE WHICH HAS SHROUDED THE DIM PAST FROM THE BRIGHT PRESENT.... AND, PLOP! WE ARE RIGHT DAB-SMACK INTO A CHRISTMAS YESTERYEAR! PLEASANTRIES OF OLD AGAIN SURROUND US. OF COURSE, THEY'RE ONLY MERRY MEMORIES....

'TWAS INDEED PEACE, CONTENTMENT AND GENUINE FRIENDLINESS _THE REAL CHRISTMAS SPIRIT. THE FRAGRANT ODOR OF BURNING WOOD AND BALSAM MINGLED DELICIOUSLY WITH THE SMELL OF COFFEE, FOR A POT OF IT ALWAYS BREWED _READY FOR ANYONE WHO WOULD STOP BY.....
YES, THOSE NEIGHBORS WERE SO GOOD... AND THE OLD NEIGHBORHOOD WAS SO NICE... AND THE ENTIRE SURROUNDINGS WERE SO PLEASANT.
THERE WERE THE SNOWY STREETS DIMLY LIGHTED WITH THE CORNER LAMPS....... AND DARK BUNDLES OF PEOPLE SAT IN CUTTERS AS THEY DASHED SMOOTHLY DOWN THE STREET.... AND THERE WERE ITS OLD-FASHIONED STORES..... ONE OF THEM MAMA WENT TO.... WE WENT WITH HER! 'TWAS A NICE OLD PLACE. ESPECIALLY NICE WERE THE JARS FULL OF COLORED CANDIES ON THE COUNTER.
'TWAS LIKE THAT AT OUR HOUSE, TOO!
THAT WAS THE STORE WE TRUDGED TO ON THAT SPARKLING NIGHT OF YESTERYEAR... A CHRISTMAS EVE WE REMEMBER DISTINCTLY.
THE STORE WE WENT TO WAS ON A BUSY STREET, NOT FAR FROM OUR NEIGHBORHOOD! THERE WAS THE HEADY SMELL OF THE PONDEROUS OLD RED COFFEE GRINDER _ THE HEAVY AROMA OF SPICES IN OPEN BINS _ THE FRAGRANCE OF GINGER AND CINNAMON AND OVERHEAD HUNG PAPER BAGS ON HOOKS AND LANTERNS AND MITTENS AND WHAT NOT. BEST OF ALL, THE GROCER GAVE US A SACK OF PEPPERMINT.... and...

THEN... AS AN ADDED TREAT FOR CHRISTMAS, HE SEARCHED THE MURKY BRINE OF A YAWNING BARREL TO BRING FORTH SOME BIG DILL PICKLES, FOR US, ON A LONG WOODEN LADLE. EVEN ON CHRISTMAS EVE A PICKLE TASTED GOOD! OUT ON THE BUSY STREET WERE MANY PEOPLE ....BUSY, TOO!
WE LEFT THE STORE! OUTSIDE, THE AIR CRACKED WITH THE BELOW-ZERO FROST. EVERYTHING WAS A PICTURE OF SILVER FROST. LIGHTS FROM THE STORE WINDOWS GLINTED YELLOW ON THE SNOW. OUR NOSES WERE GETTING COLORFUL, TOO..... A CHERRY RED! IT WAS A VERY BEAUTIFUL CHRISTMAS EVE, INCREDIBLE HAPPINESS WAS HEAPED UPON THAT LOVABLE OLD-FASHIONED COMMUNITY WITH ITS EASYGOING SPIRITS AND ITS SIMPLE DELIGHTS. SLEIGHBELLS MADE THE AIR DANCE! A JOLLY MAN SOLD HOT CHESTNUTS AND LAMPLIGHTS FLICKERED. THERE WAS SOMETHING RICH ABOUT THAT OLD-TIME SIMPLICITY.

YES, IN THOSE DAYS CHRISTMASTIME
WAS MORE SIMPLE AND THE WORLD
AROUND US WAS SO STILL ....
AT NIGHT, TOO; AND SO DARK AND QUIET THAT THE ONLY LIGHT IN
IT WERE THE LITTLE GOLDEN FLAMES OF CANDLES AND THE LITTLE
SILVER FLAMES OF STARS, ALMOST LIKE THAT FIRST SILENT NIGHT....
WHEN THE CHRIST
CHILD WAS BORN!
THAT PARTICULAR CHRISTMAS EVE
IN OUR OLD NEIGHBORHOOD WAS
ALMOST SUCH A SILENT NIGHT ....

'TWAS ALMOST SILENT. NOW AND THEN A BOB-SLED OR A CUTTER PASSED, ITS HARNESS JINGLING AND WE HEARD GOOD PEOPLE SINGING HYMNS ......
and then, ...
'TWAS SILENT!.... A WONDERFUL CHRISTMAS EVE! WE REACHED HOME. THE LIGHT IN THE KITCHEN WAS WARMINGLY INVITING. THE WOODSHED DOOR, WHICH HAD BEEN LOCKED, WAS OPEN ... WE NOTICED IT!
WEBS OF SMOKE SPUN TOWARD THE STARS FROM THE CHIMNEYS. INTO THE KITCHEN WE TRAMPLED, GLAD TO BE IN IT AGAIN! THE SENSE OF BEING SHUT IN FROM THE WORLD WAS SUCH A DELIGHTFUL FEELING. WE HAD NOTHING AGAINST THE WORLD, SO BEAUTIFUL 'TWAS OUTSIDE ... BUT OUR CHERRY-RED NOSES AND FROZEN TOES HAD SOMETHING AGAINST IT .... JUST TEMPORARILY!
ONCE IN THE WARM SNUGNESS OF THE HOUSE, WE DISCOVERED THAT THE PARLOR DOOR WAS LOCKED! THAT MEANT PAPA HAD A CHRISTMAS TREE IN THE WOODSHED! AND HE WAS TRIMMING IT! WE WERE CONVINCED WHEN WE HEARD ORNAMENTS FALL!

WE CANNOT DESCRIBE WHAT TOOK PLACE IN THE PARLOR BECAUSE WE DIDN'T SEE IT! WE TRIED TO LINGER IN THE KITCHEN WHERE MAMA MADE GOODIES, DELICIOUS ENOUGH TO MAKE A DICTIONARY LOOK BLANK WHEN WE TRIED TO FIND WORDS TO DESCRIBE THE FLAVORS... *BUT*, OFF TO BED WE HAD TO GO...RELUCTANTLY!

WE'LL NEVER FORGET THAT OLD KITCHEN!

WE HAD A SUSPICION THAT MAMA WANTED US OFF TO BED SO SHE COULD HELP PAPA! ANYWAY, SISTER SLEPT DOWNSTAIRS AND WE, UPSTAIRS. AFTER WE SAID OUR PRAYERS WE WENT TO THE WINDOW AND LOOKED OUT, UP AT THE STARLIT SKY. ONE STAR WAS MUCH BRIGHTER. IT SEEMED TO US TO BE THE STAR OF BETHLEHEM.....

YES, ...

PERHAPS IT WAS THAT GREAT, GALLANT LEADING STAR WE SAW IN THE SKY THAT NIGHT...OR MAYBE IT WAS JUST BECAUSE IT WAS **CHRISTMAS EVE!**

CHRISTMAS MORNING SPARKLED..... BUT, WHAT HAPPENED ON THAT DAY IS STILL A MYSTERY. THERE WERE TOYS AND A THOUSAND MILLION JOYS, ENOUGH TO MAKE US FORGET.....

But,

WHEN THE TREE WAS LIGHTED IN THE OLD PARLOR, 'TWAS THEN THAT WE STARTED TO REMEMBER AGAIN... AND WE CAPTURED A CHERISHED MEMORY...

ON THAT NIGHT AFTER THE NIGHT BEFORE CHRISTMAS!

AND SO, ONCE AGAIN WE HAVE TAKEN A JOURNEY INTO YESTERYEAR, "SURROUNDED" IN THE OLD CHILDHOOD NEIGHBORHOOD BY GOOD FOLKS...JUST LIKE YOU AN' YOU AN' YOU! AS SOON AS WE REMEMBERED HOW OLD THE MEMORIES WERE, OUR STROLL ENDED! BUT, IN ANOTHER YEAR WE'LL BE ANXIOUS AGAIN TO SCAMPER DOWN CHRISTMAS MEMORY LANE!

Cherished and Shared of Old

SUSAN GLASPELL

Though we know that never a longing mortal gains life best—Oh, better it is to pray for part in what we cherished and shared of old than fail to remember.—Sappho

Thank goodness for the snow," thought Addie Morrison, as she watched the two children racing round the barn. And she was thinking it was nice there were some things that were everywhere—most everywhere: like sun and rain, like the wind and the snow, so's when you were sent far from your home there were these things—like the stars—to make you feel a little more at home in a distant land.

"Not a soul here they ever knew before," she would think of these two little Dutch children she'd taken into her home. They were warm now at night—not wandering on a road. They weren't hungry now—mercy no, she'd seen to that, but what are they thinking, she'd wonder, as at times they'd sit there so gravely. She wished they'd do more things they shouldn't, for when you're too good you must be a little afraid. She hadn't been able to stand the pictures in the papers—so many tired children waiting to get back home. Her daughter Emmey . . . was working for little ones who had been turned out into the world. "Mother dear," she wrote, "I can't get home this Christmas—just can't. But I could send you two children for whom you could make a Christmas the way you used to for me and Jack. You'll be so sorry for Johanna and Piet, and come to love them. . . ."

So once more there were children on the old Morrison place, but could she make a happy Christmas for this little girl and boy bereft of their own? She could say "Merry Christmas," but could she make their hearts glad? And what is Christmas if there is not warmth within?

She didn't even know what they were used to for Christmas. She wished, for just five minutes, she could talk to their mother. "What would they like?" she'd ask. And their mother would reply—eagerly, so anxious: "Oh, if you would give them. . ." But this mother couldn't speak up for her children—struck down trying to hurry them to safety.

Germans did that. The Schultzes were Germans—over there in their fine house on the hill. And so her heart hardened anew against Emma Schultz—and that was good, for she found it not so easy to hate Emma at Christmas.

Never a Christmas they hadn't shared—all those years they were growing up. In this very kitchen they'd hung around sniffing and tasting. And when they weren't here they were at the Schultzes'. She had two homes—her own and Schultzes'. And Emma had two—her own and the Morrisons'.

And then they had to act like that. Just to get a piece of land that didn't belong to them at all they'd fought John Morrison, best friend they'd had since they came—greenhorns—where the Morrisons had been since first there were white men in Iowa! Not to her dying day would she forget her father's face that late afternoon he came back from town, and standing by this very table said: "Well, they've won. The court has given them the strip. Don't ask me why. I don't know why. But I do know this. They've won the land—but they've lost the Morrisons. Never again—do you hear me, Addie?—never again can a Morrison be friend to a Schultz."

Oh, she heard him all right, and never forgot. How could she forget, when she saw him change from that day? The land wasn't so very important. But the defeat—bitter words spoken—from that day he began to brood, until soon people were saying: "Why Addie, seems like your father is beginning to fail."

But Emil Schultz—he didn't fail. As the Morrisons began to have less and less, the Schultzes had more and more. Emma Schultz's land-grabbing father lived on till just last year—and many a snow had fallen since they carried John Morrison to the last land he would know. So a fine daughter she was—letting into her heart memories of those long ago Christmases with Emma Schultz. Memories were tricky things—come Christmastime. Maybe it was because you went on doing the same things. You made the cranberry sauce, trimmed the tree—

doing alone the little things you'd done with someone else—with the dearest friend you'd ever had.

For no one had ever taken Emma's place. Who could take the place of the friend with whom you'd shared all those good years of your life? Emma helped her make all her wedding things. Emma was there when her first baby was born. She'd named that daughter Emma. Later she'd thought of changing it—but not easy to change a name, and anyway she had an aunt named Emma—she got around it that way. And Walter. Emma was to have married Addie's brother Walter. But Walter went away to war . . . and he never came back. And they had comforted each other then.

Yes, laughter and sorrow they had shared. And how divided now! That fought-over land connected the Morrison and Schultz farms. Connected only to divide. It wasn't land—it was a gulf, a gulf that had widened with the years. . . .

The smells of Christmas brought Emma close to her—Christmas smells trying to make her betray the legacy of hate to which she had been so bitterly loyal. "And what if we did get many a Christmas dinner together," she thought. Remember the words—those very words they spoke!

Yes—the words. How cruel—and again how blessed—were words. They could carry testimony of love, the sympathy that brought heart closer to heart and warmed the world. And they could blast and wound and kill like those contraptions of the devil man used against man in war. And their life was as long as the life of man.

Longer. For the men who had fought for that land were gone now—her father and Emma's. Walter was gone, and Addie's husband. Her children were in homes of their own and she lived on here at the old place . . . and over there on the hill, in her fine new house, lived Emma Schultz. She had a frigidaire, they said—a vacuum and everything to make life easy. . . . How she'd laugh if she knew poor old Addie Morrison was thinking of the days they'd made the Christmas candy together—remembering how Emma's stocking hung at the Morrisons', and Addie's at the Schultzes'.

"Come in and get warm!" she called to the children. "Stamp hard! Shake!" she cried gaily. They got in a mix-up getting off Piet's ski pants. . . . Piet laughed out loud and Johanna smiled—her grave little smile that seemed to be feeling its way. "It will take time," Addie told herself. Tomorrow they'd have their presents—sleds and skates, toys and new caps and mufflers and mittens. . . .

Once she'd heard them break out in laughter that came because it couldn't help itself—how happy she'd be, as if a little of the weight of misery had lifted from the world. Perhaps Christmas could do that. That was what Christmas was for. She wanted them to be happy as she hadn't wanted anything in years. That would be her Christmas present—a smile not uncertain, a laugh that was happy clear to the inside. . . .

Well, if that little fellow wasn't edging up to the cookie jar. Good! You must think it's your house when you go after the cookie jar. Johanna said, in her new careful English, "Thank you," for the cookie; little Piet said something she didn't understand, but he smiled and she knew it was "Thank you." What funny little cookies the Schultzes used to make for Christmas. Cut in all sorts of shapes—a rabbit, a star, a St. Nicholas and something called a grampus, and supposed to be for the bad child, but it had currants and nuts in it just the same, so who cared? Perhaps Johanna and Piet were used to cookies like that. Yes, Emma might know more than she did about what these children were used to. But Emma—warm in a fine sealskin coat—what did she care?

"Oh—pret-ty," she heard Johanna murmur, and turned to find her fingering a length of red ribbon that was to be tied on the tree. Addie stood stock-still watching her, for the little girl's fingers moved over the bright stuff so wistfully, as if—as if she had once loved something like this. "Oh you poor little thing," she thought, in a new wave of sympathy and tenderness—and anger too. All the little fineries left behind. Only what you needed—not the pretty things to make life gay.

"Time to dress ourselves up for Christmas," she said, slipping the bright broad ribbon under the collar of Johanna's sweater and making a fine red bow.

And then she began to laugh—Emma running after a pig, trying to catch the pig to tie a red ribbon around his neck. That was one of the crazy things they did together, dressing up the animals for Christmas. Well, Emma caught the pig, but fell down doing it and Emma and pig rolled over and over together—the pig squirming and Emma clutching. Addie could see them now and she went on laughing, until the children, thinking there must be something very funny indeed, politely joined in.

The snow continued to fall softly, knowing it was Christmas and the world should be white, and after the dinner things were cleared away Addie wondered whether they'd like to be bundled up and go out again. That was the trouble—it was still hard to know for sure what they would like, for it wasn't their house yet.

But suddenly it was! What in the world were they looking at out that window—dancing up and down, catching hold of each other and squealing and pointing?

Oh—dear. Now what? For there he was—that miserable Schultz dog who came bounding over as if he didn't know a Schultz shouldn't come to the Morrisons'. She started for the door to go chase him away but the children thought she was going to let him in, and they were right upon her, all excited and happy—natural—for the first time they really were children. And all because that ugly Schultz dog—for some crazy reason called Doc—was standing there wagging his tail as if waiting for them to come out and play with him.

"Bad dog," she said. "German. Bad German dog"—though she knew she shouldn't be doing this.

But they didn't care. It didn't seem to make any difference to them that Doc was German. And then Addie knew. It wasn't only the ribbons and the toys had been left behind. The dog had been left behind too. . . .

"We'll get a dog, she said. "A nice dog. This is the homeliest dog ever lived." And Doc was a very funny-looking dog. He wasn't any kind of dog—just Doc. He had a bulldog face and crooked legs, but he was sort of a dog of all nations, and Addie knew in her heart that the kindness of all nations came together in Doc, and that Doc was a good dog. But he was a Schultz.

She tried to interest them in the dog they would have, but they wanted Doc and wanted him right now; and as Addie saw that first flare-up of joy begin to die down into disappointment, of course she couldn't stand it and there began a mad gay scramble to get them into their clothes so they could rush out and play with Doc Schultz.

Then she remembered they were used to having dogs draw things—pictures of Holland always had dogs drawing little carts—so she hurried into the shut-up front room, where the presents waited in secret, to get the Christmas sled—for might as well be killed for a sheep as a lamb, she thought.

Oh, they were so delighted! They could scarcely wait to get out—and then they were all in a scramble together, Doc jumping on them and waving his silly tail—and for goodness sakes if the dog didn't seem to be grinning—and the children were laughing and screaming and they all went tearing away together. And Addie Morrison sat there thinking it was strange—so very strange—that their first happy moment on the Morrison place came through Emma Schultz. She sat there alone remembering her dogs and Emma's—new sleds—and other mad scrambles in the Christmas snow.

Emma Schultz was remembering something herself. She was again a little girl not eight—new to America, a greenhorn. And the children at school stared and laughed at her because she talked funny and didn't know their ways. But little Addie Morrison—so pretty then—came up and hooked her arm through Emma's and said: "You and me, let's us be friends." More than anything else in the world she would like to walk over to Addie Morrison now, open the kitchen door just as she used to, and say, "You and me, let's us be friends." At Christmas it was so hard not to remember. . . .

Emma was the one to do something for these children, for who could know better than she what it was to be a child among things not familiar. She was putting in a big jar the *Lebkuchen,* German Christmas cookies she made every year. She wouldn't have had the heart to make them this year, but her mother hadn't many Christmases left and clung to the things she was used to. Next week Emma's Sunday-school class would come for their party, and they'd have these cookies and their presents. But it was lonely here today.

Ten thousand times she'd wished that land in the bottom of the sea. What is land, compared to the love of friends? How gladly she would have given it back. It had changed things for the Schultzes. Her father grew hard after that and wanted to make money and didn't care about friends. And she herself had to pretend she didn't care. . . . But it had been lonely business, and at Christmas especially she knew there still lived in her heart all she and Addie had loved together, dear things shared. She'd like to cross that strip—and abolish it in crossing—open the kitchen door and see if there wasn't something she could do for these little children against whom a wicked wrong had been worked. But what nonsense. You couldn't change the way things were. "Emma! I hear Doc barking," her mother called out to her. "He wants to come in."

She opened her own kitchen door and yes—there stood Doc. But—what in the world? He was all decorated for Christmas. Red ribbon was wound round his collar and tied in a big gay bow. Now who could have done that?

And suddenly Emma Schultz sat down—so sure there was only one person in the world could have sent Doc home decorated for Christmas. She and Addie used to do that together. The dogs always had their big red Christmas bows. Addie had not forgotten. Oh, she had sent a message saying she remembered. And Emma Schultz began hurrying fast as she could—getting the cookies—presents for those she had for her Sunday-school class—for couldn't she get others for them? Filling a big basket, hurrying into her boots, her coat, and out into the snow. It was Christmas! She ran across the strip giving it scarcely a thought, so eager to get to the Morrisons'.

But at the kitchen door she paused. So many years . . . Then she knocked, and Addie opened the door.

"Why—why Emma Schultz," she said, as if she didn't know what to say.

"Merry Christmas, Addie," said Emma—timidly, bravely.

"Why—why—" And then all of a sudden Addie cried, "Merry Christmas yourself!" and swiftly added, "For pity sakes come right in out of the snow!"

A little later they were all sitting round the kitchen stove, nibbling the cookies Emma had brought, Emma and Addie drinking tea and the children their cocoa—so cozy in the Morrison kitchen. Yes, Johanna and Piet knew cookies like these, and great fun they had picking out now a new moon, now a little man, Johanna hugging the doll Emma had brought and Piet dangling the baby panda.

"Emma!" Addie burst out with a laughter, "do you remember the pig?"

While they were laughing came a barking and scratching at the door and Johanna and Piet ran to let in their friend Doc. As the children were busy brushing him off, Emma said, very low, "Oh, Addie, when he came home all fixed up for Christmas and I knew you had remembered, were telling me you remembered."

Addie had been sitting with her back to Doc. She turned now, and saw that the bow she had tied on Johanna at this moment adorned Emma's dog Doc. And Emma thought she had done this. A Schultz thought a Morrison had made the first move. Ah, there was danger in that moment—danger the world has faced time and again. Old bitter loyalties—resentments of many years—right there, ready to rush in. But something else came flooding into that moment: It was the children had done this. The children whom hate had driven here—brought love. How strange that this could be. Like a miracle it seemed.

She was afraid she was going to cry, so when Doc came sniffing up to the stove she said, almost crossly, "Why, Emma Schultz—that dog's hungry."

"I'll tell you, children," she went on, "what do you say we give him our beef stew, for tomorrow we'll have turkey."

Doc knew it was to be for him and was dancing all around, his big bow bobbing. "Say Merry Christmas!" cried Addie, holding high the plate. Doc waved a hearty "Merry Christmas"—and they all watched Doc Schultz devour the Morrison stew. The children clapped their hands at the speed with which he cleaned the plate. Emma and Addie smiled at each other—so much alive and warm between them. Dogs of other years were wearing their Christmas bows and cleaning the plate. In a changing world of many sorrows it can be sad to remember alone. But when friends share dear memories—a fire in the cold, light in the darkness.

And right there the children began a great clatter, running round in circles with Doc. Why, they weren't a bit afraid—for all the world as if they knew something had happened there amongst them. Whether they knew it or not, it was true—how blessed and true—that fear flew out through the window when love came in by the door.

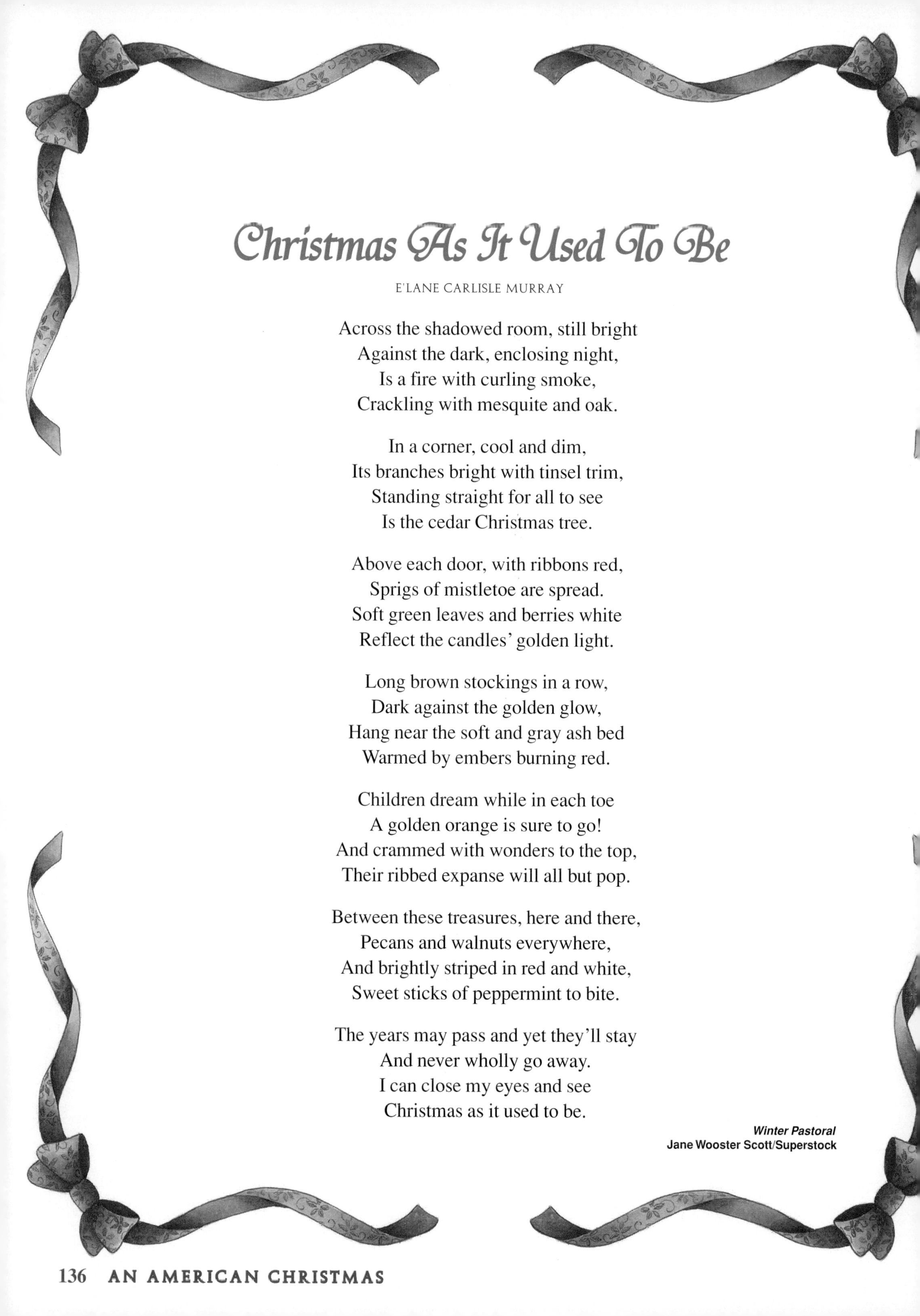

Christmas As It Used To Be

E'LANE CARLISLE MURRAY

Across the shadowed room, still bright
Against the dark, enclosing night,
Is a fire with curling smoke,
Crackling with mesquite and oak.

In a corner, cool and dim,
Its branches bright with tinsel trim,
Standing straight for all to see
Is the cedar Christmas tree.

Above each door, with ribbons red,
Sprigs of mistletoe are spread.
Soft green leaves and berries white
Reflect the candles' golden light.

Long brown stockings in a row,
Dark against the golden glow,
Hang near the soft and gray ash bed
Warmed by embers burning red.

Children dream while in each toe
A golden orange is sure to go!
And crammed with wonders to the top,
Their ribbed expanse will all but pop.

Between these treasures, here and there,
Pecans and walnuts everywhere,
And brightly striped in red and white,
Sweet sticks of peppermint to bite.

The years may pass and yet they'll stay
And never wholly go away.
I can close my eyes and see
Christmas as it used to be.

Winter Pastoral
Jane Wooster Scott/Superstock

Winter Pastoral
© Wooster Scott

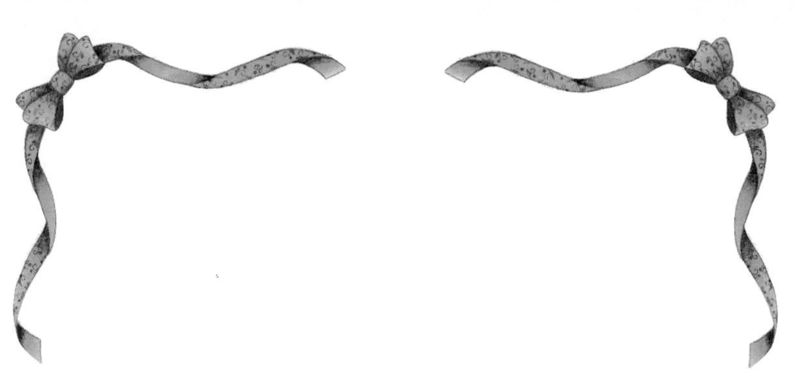

Christmas INSPIRATION

Ancient tidings
told again,
"Peace on earth, good
will toward men!"
Precious now as
they were then—

This is Christmas!

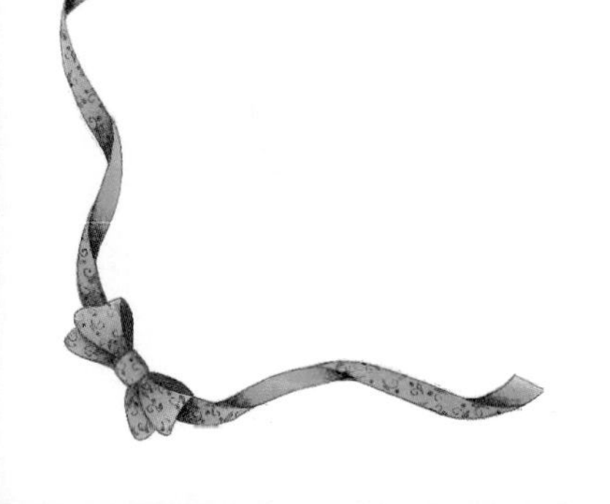

Home for Christmas
Linda Nelson Stocks

Rise Up, Shepherd, and Follow

TRADITIONAL

fol - low; Leave your ewes and leave your rams,
Rise up, shep - herd, and fol - low. Fol - low,
fol - low, Rise up, shep - herd, and fol - low.
Fol - low the Star of Beth - le - hem, Rise up, shep- herd, and fol - low.

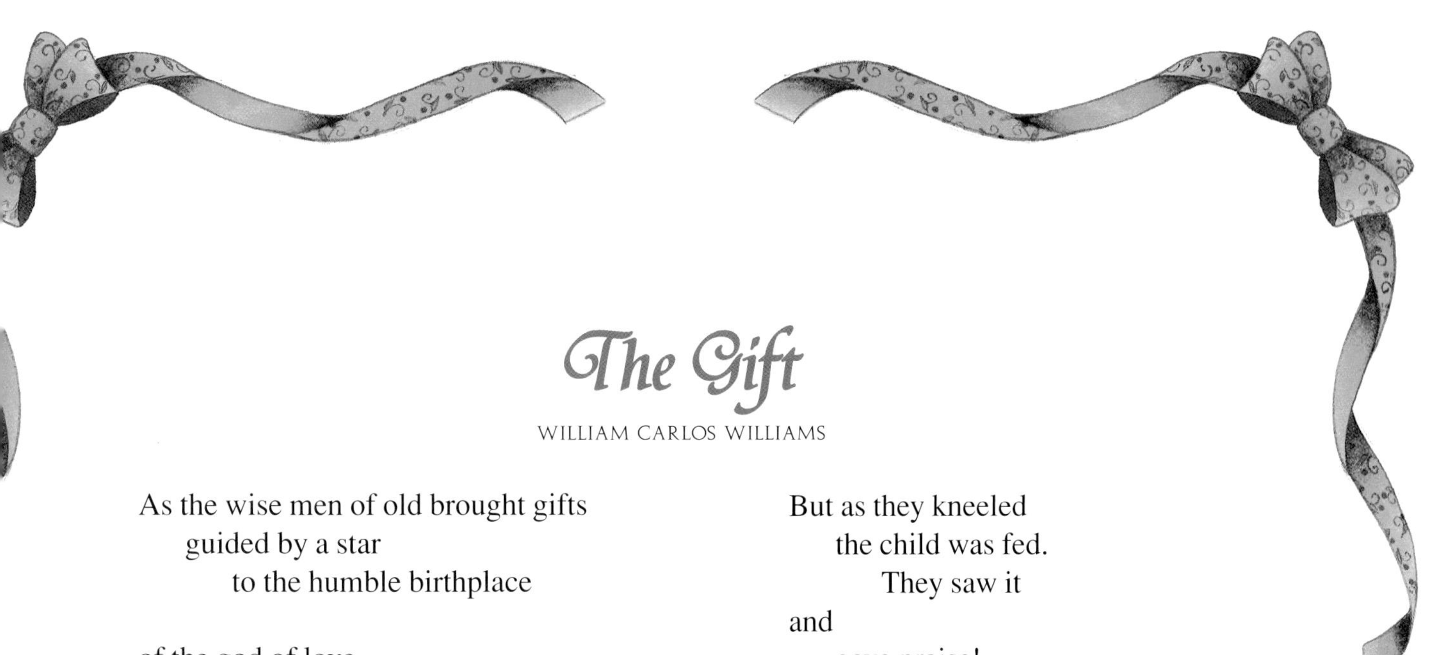

The Gift

WILLIAM CARLOS WILLIAMS

As the wise men of old brought gifts
guided by a star
to the humble birthplace

of the god of love,
the devils
as an old print shows
retreated in confusion.

What could a baby know
of gold ornaments
or frankincense and myrrh,
of priestly robes
and devout genuflections?

But the imagination
knows all stories
before they are told
and knows the truth of this one
past all defection.

The rich gifts
so unsuitable for a child
though devoutly proffered,
stood for all that love can bring.

The men were old
how could they know
of a mother's needs
or a child's
appetite?

But as they kneeled
the child was fed.
They saw it
and
gave praise!

A miracle
had taken place,
hard gold to love,
a mother's milk!
Before
their wondering eyes.

The ass brayed
the cattle lowed.
It was their nature.

All men by their nature give praise.
It is all
they can do.

The very devils
by their flight gave praise.
What is death,
beside this?

Nothing. The wise men
came with gifts
and bowed down
to worship
this perfection.

Winter Chelsea, Vermont
Dick Dietrich Photography

The Coming of the Prince

EUGENE FIELD

Whirr-r-r! Whirr-r-r! Whirr-r-r! said the wind, and it tore through the streets of the city that Christmas Eve, turning umbrellas inside out, driving the snow in fitful gusts before it, creaking the rusty signs and shutters, and playing every kind of rude prank it could think of.

"How cold your breath is tonight!" said Barbara, with a shiver, as she drew her tattered little shawl the closer around her benumbed body.

"Whirr-r-r! whirr-r-r! whirr-r-r!" answered the wind; "but why are you out in this storm? You should be at home by the warm fire."

"I have no home," said Barbara; and then she sighed bitterly, and something like a tiny pearl came in the corner of one of her sad blue eyes.

But the wind did not hear her answer, for it had hurried up the street to throw a handful of snow in the face of an old man who was struggling along with a huge basket of good things on each arm.

"Why are you not at the cathedral?" asked a snowflake, as it lighted on Barbara's shoulder. "I heard grand music, and saw beautiful lights there as I floated down from the sky a moment ago."

"What are they doing at the cathedral?" inquired Barbara.

"Why, haven't you heard?" exclaimed the snowflake. "I supposed everybody knew that the prince was coming tomorrow."

"Surely enough; this is Christmas Eve," said Barbara, "and the prince will come tomorrow."

Barbara remembered that her mother had told her about the prince, how beautiful and good and kind and gentle he was, and how he loved the little children; but her mother was dead now, and there was none to tell Barbara of the prince and his coming—none but the little snowflake.

"I should like to see the prince," said Barbara, "for I have heard he was very beautiful and good."

"That he is," said the snowflake. "I have never seen him, but I heard the pines and the firs singing about him as I floated over the forest tonight."

"Whirr-r-r! whirr-r-r!" cried the wind, returning boisterously to where Barbara stood. "I've been looking for you everywhere, little snowflake! So come with me."

And without any further ado, the wind seized upon the snowflake and hurried it along the street and led it a merry dance through the icy air of the winter night.

Barbara trudged on through the snow and looked in at the bright things in the shop windows. The glitter of the lights and the sparkle of the vast array of beautiful Christmas toys quite dazzled her. A strange mingling of admiration, regret, and envy filled the poor little creature's heart.

"Much as I may yearn to have them, it cannot be," she said to herself, "yet I may feast my eyes upon them."

"Go away from here!" said a harsh voice. "How can the rich people see all my fine things if you stand before the window? Be off with you, you miserable little beggar!"

It was the shopkeeper, and he gave Barbara a savage box on the ear that sent her reeling into the deeper snowdrifts of the gutter.

Presently she came to a large house where there seemed to be much mirth and festivity. The shutters were thrown open, and through the windows Barbara could see a beautiful Christmas tree in the center of a spacious room—a beautiful Christmas tree ablaze with red and green lights, and heavy with toys and stars and glass balls and other beautiful things that children love. There was a merry throng around the tree, and the children were smiling and gleeful, and all in that house seemed content and happy. Barbara heard them singing, and their song was about the prince who was to come on the morrow.

"This must be the house where the prince will stop," thought Barbara. "How I would like to see his face and hear his voice!—yet what would he care for me, a 'miserable little beggar?'"

So Barbara crept on through the storm, shivering and disconsolate, yet thinking of the prince.

"Where are you going?" she asked of the wind as it overtook her.

"To the cathedral," laughed the wind. "The

great people are flocking there, and I will have a merry time amongst them, ha, ha, ha!"

And with laughter the wind whirled away and chased the snow toward the cathedral.

"It is there, then, that the prince will come," thought Barbara. "It is a beautiful place, and the people will pay him homage there. Perhaps I shall see him if I go there."

So she went to the cathedral. Many folk were there in their richest apparel, and the organ rolled out its grand music, and the people sang wondrous songs, and the priests made eloquent prayers; and the music, and the songs, and the prayers were all about the prince and his expected coming. The throng that swept in and out of the great edifice talked always of the prince, the prince, the prince, until Barbara really loved him very much for all the gentle words she heard the people say of him.

"Please, can I go and sit inside?" inquired Barbara of the sexton.

"No!" said the sexton gruffly, for this was an important occasion with the sexton, and he had no idea of wasting words on a beggar child.

"But I will be very good and quiet," pleaded Barbara. "Please may I not see the prince?"

"I have said no, and I mean it," retorted the sexton. "What have you for the prince, or what cares the prince for you? Out with you, and don't be blocking up the doorway! So the sexton gave Barbara an angry push, and the child fell halfway down the icy steps of the cathedral. She began to cry. Some great people were entering the cathedral at the time, and they laughed to see her falling.

"Have you seen the prince?" inquired a snowflake, alighting on Barbara's cheek. It was the same little snowflake that had clung to her shawl an hour ago, when the wind came galloping along on his boisterous search.

"Ah, no!" sighed Barbara in tears; "but what cares the prince for me?"

"Do not speak so bitterly," said the little snowflake. "Go to the forest and you shall see him, for the prince always comes through the forest to the city."

Despite the cold, and her bruises, and her tears, Barbara smiled. In the forest she could behold the prince coming on his way; and he would not see her, for she would hide among the trees and vines.

"Whirr-r-r, whirr-r-r!" It was the mischievous, romping wind once more; and it fluttered Barbara's tattered shawl, and set her hair to streaming in every direction, and swept the snowflake from her cheek and sent it spinning through the air.

Barbara trudged toward the forest. When she came to the city gate the watchman stopped her, and held his big lantern in her face, and asked her who she was and where she was going.

"I am Barbara, and I am going into the forest," said she boldly.

"Into the forest?" cried the watchman. "And in this storm? No, child; you will perish!"

"But I am going to see the prince," said Barbara. "They will not let me watch for him in the church, nor in any of their pleasant homes, so I am going into the forest."

The watchman smiled sadly. He was a kindly man; he thought of his own little girl at home.

"No, you must not go to the forest," said he, "for you would perish with the cold."

But Barbara would not stay. She avoided the watchman's grasp and ran as fast as ever she could through the city gate.

"Come back, come back!" cried the watchman. "You will perish in the forest!"

But Barbara would not heed his cry. The falling snow did not stay her, nor did the cutting blast. She thought only of the prince, and she ran straightway to the forest.

"What do you see up there, O pine tree?" asked a little vine in the forest. "You lift your head among the clouds tonight, and you tremble strangely as if you saw wondrous sights."

"I see only the distant hilltops and the dark clouds," answered the pine tree. "And the wind sings of the snow king tonight; to all my questionings he says, 'Snow, snow, snow,' till I am wearied with his refrain."

"But the prince will surely come tomorrow?" inquired the tiny snowdrop that nestled close to the vine.

"Oh, yes," said the vine. "I heard the country folks talking about it as they went through the forest today, and they said that the prince would surely come on the morrow."

"What are you little folks down there talking about?" asked the pine tree.

"We are talking about the prince," said the vine.

"Yes, he is coming on the morrow," said the pine tree, "but not until the day dawns and it is still all dark in the east."

"Yes, said the fir tree, "the east is black, and only the wind and the snow issue from it."

"Keep your head out of my way!" cried the pine tree to the fir; "with your constant bobbing around I can hardly see at all."

"Take that for your bad manner," retorted the fir, slapping the pine tree savagely with one of her longest branches.

The pine tree would put up with no such treatment, so he hurled his largest cone at the fir; and for a moment or two it looked as if there were going to be a serious commotion in the forest.

"Hush!" cried the vine in a startled tone; "there is someone coming through the forest."

The pine tree and the fir stopped quarreling, and the snowdrop nestled closer to the vine, while the vine hugged the pine tree very tightly. All were greatly alarmed.

"Nonsense!" said the pine tree, in a tone of assumed bravery. "No one would venture into the forest at such an hour."

"Indeed! and why not?" cried a child's voice. "Will you not let me watch with you for the coming of the prince?"

"Will you not chop me down?" inquired the pine tree gruffly.

"Will you not tear me from my tree?" asked the vine.

"Will you not pluck my blossoms?" plaintively piped the snowdrop.

"No, of course not," said Barbara; "I have come only to watch with you for the prince."

Then Barbara told them who she was, and how cruelly she had been treated in the city, and how she longed to see the prince, who was to come on the morrow. And as she talked, the forest and all therein felt a great compassion for her.

"Lie at my feet," said the pine tree, "and I will protect you."

"Nestle close to me, and I will chafe your temples and body and limbs till they are warm," said the vine.

"Let me rest upon your cheek, and I will sing you my little songs," said the snowdrop.

And Barbara felt very grateful for all these lovely kindnesses. She rested in the velvety snow at the foot of the pine tree, and the vine chafed her body and limbs, and the little flower sang sweet songs to her.

"Whirr-r-r! whirr-r-r!" There was that noisy wind again, but this time it was gentler than it had been in the city.

"Here you are, my little Barbara," said the wind, in kindly tones. "I have brought you the little snowflake. I am glad you came away from the city, for the people are proud and haughty there; oh, but I will have my fun with them!"

Then, having dropped the little snowflake on Barbara's cheek, the wind whisked off to the city again. And we can imagine that it played rare pranks with the proud, haughty folk on its return; for the wind, as you know, is no respecter of persons.

"Dear Barbara," said the snowflake, "I will watch with thee for the coming of the prince."

And Barbara was glad, for she loved the little snowflake that was so pure and innocent and gentle.

"Tell us, O pine tree," cried the vine, "what do you see in the east? Has the prince yet entered the forest?"

"The east is full of black clouds," said the pine tree, "and the winds that hurry to the hilltops sing of the snow."

"But the city is full of brightness," said the fir. "I can see the lights in the cathedral, and I can hear wondrous music about the prince and his coming."

"Yes, they are singing of the prince in the cathedral," said Barbara sadly.

"But we shall see him first," whispered the vine reassuringly.

"Yes, the prince will come through the forest," said the little snowdrop gleefully.

"Fear not, dear Barbara, we shall behold the prince in all his glory," cried the snowflake.

Then all at once there was a strange hubbub in the forest; for it was midnight, and the spirits came from their hiding places to prowl about and to disport themselves. Barbara beheld them all in great wonder and trepidation, for she had never before seen the spirits of the forest, although she had often heard of them. It was a marvelous sight.

"Fear nothing," whispered the vine to Barbara, "fear nothing, for they dare not touch you."

The antics of the wood-spirits continued but an hour; for then a cock crowed, and immediately thereat, with a wondrous scurrying, the elves and the gnomes and the other grotesque spirits sought their abiding places in the caves and in the hollow trunks and under the loose bark of the trees. Then it was very quiet once more in the forest.

"It is very cold," said Barbara, "my hands and my feet are like ice."

Then the pine tree and the fir shook down the snow from their broad boughs, and the snow fell upon Barbara and covered her like a white mantle.

"You will be warm now," said the vine, kissing Barbara's forehead. And Barbara smiled.

Then the snowdrop sang a lullaby about the moss that loved the violet. And Barbara said, "I am going to sleep; will you wake me when the prince comes through the forest?"

And they said they would. So Barbara fell asleep.

"The bells in the city are ringing merrily," said the fir, "and the music in the cathedral is louder and more beautiful than before. Can it be that the prince has already come into the city?"

"No," cried the pine tree, "look to the east and see the Christmas day a-dawning! The prince is coming, and his pathway is through the forest."

The storm had ceased. Snow lay upon all the earth. The hills, the forest, the city, and the meadows were white with the robe the storm-king had thrown over them. Content with his wondrous work, the storm-king himself had fled to his far northern home before the dawn of the Christmas day. Everything was bright and sparkling and beautiful. And most beautiful was the great hymn of praise the forest sang that Christmas morning,—the pine trees and the firs and the vines and the snow-flowers that sang of the prince and of his promised coming.

"Wake up, little one," cried the vine, "for the prince is coming!"

But Barbara slept; she did not hear the vine's soft calling nor the lofty music of the forest.

A little snowbird flew down from the fir tree's bough and perched upon the vine, and caroled in Barbara's ear of the Christmas morning and of the coming of the prince. But Barbara slept; she did not hear the carol of the bird.

"Alas!" sighed the vine. "Barbara will not awaken, and the prince is coming."

Then the vine and the snowdrop wept, and the pine tree and the fir were very sad.

The prince came through the forest clad in royal raiment and wearing a golden crown. Angels came with him, and the forest sang a great hymn unto the prince, such a hymn as had never before been heard on earth. The prince came to the sleeping child and smiled upon her and called her by name.

"Barbara, my little one," said the prince, "awaken, and come with me."

Then Barbara opened her eyes and beheld the prince. And it seemed as if a new life had come to her, for there was warmth in her body and a flush upon her cheeks and a light in her eyes that were divine. And she was clothed no longer in rags, but in white flowing raiment; and upon the soft brown hair there was a crown like those which angels wear. And as Barbara arose and went to the prince, the little snowflake fell from her cheek upon her bosom, and forthwith became a pearl more precious than all other jewels upon the earth.

And the prince took Barbara in his arms and blessed her, and turning round about, returned with the little child unto His home, while the forest and the sky and the angels sang a wondrous song.

The city waited for the prince, but He did not come. None knew of the glory of the forest that Christmas morning, nor of the new life that came to little Barbara.

Come thou, dear Prince, oh, come to us this holy Christmas time! Come to the busy marts of earth, the quiet homes, the noisy streets, the humble lanes; come to us all, and with Thy love touch every human heart, that we may know that love, and in its blessed peace bear charity to all mankind!

Christmas Once Is Christmas Still

PHILLIPS BROOKS

The silent skies are full of speech
For who hath ears to hear;
The winds are whispering each to each,
The moon is calling to the beech,
And stars their sacred mission teach,
Of Faith, and Love, and Fear.

But once the sky its silence broke,
And song o'erflowed the earth,
The midnight air with glory shook.
And angels mortal language spoke.
When God our human nature took,
In Christ the Saviour's birth.

And Christmas once is Christmas still;
The gates through which He came,
And forests wild and murmuring rill,
And fruitful field and breezy hill,
And all that else the wide world fill,
Are vocal with His name.

Shall we not listen while they sing
This latest Christmas morn,
And music hear in everything,
And faithful lives in tribute bring
To the great song which greets the King
Who comes when Christ is born?

The sky can still remember
The earliest Christmas morn,
When in the cold December
The Saviour Christ was born;
And still in darkness clouded,
And still in noonday light,
It feels its far depths crowded
With angels fair and bright.

O never failing splendor!
O never silent song!
Still keep the green earth tender,
Still keep the gray earth strong;
Still keep the brave earth dreaming
Of deeds that shall be done,
While children's lives come streaming
Like sunbeams from the sun.

No star unfolds its glory,
No trumpet's wind is blown,
But tells the Christmas story
In music of its own.
No eager strife of mortals,
In busy fields or town,
But sees the open portals
Through which the Christ
came down.

O angels sweet and splendid,
Throng in our hearts, and sing
The wonders which attended
The coming of the King;
Till we, too, boldly pressing
Where once the angel trod,
Climb Bethlehem's hill of blessing,
And find the Son of God.

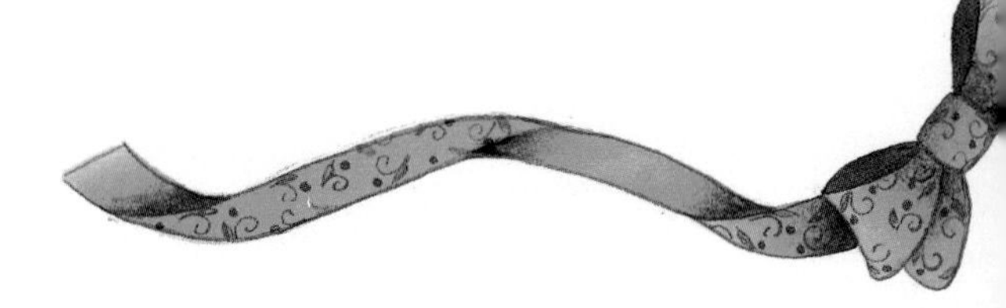

RUGEN'S
NOTIONS
TOYS

The Christmas Story

LUKE'S ACCOUNT OF CHRIST'S GLORIOUS BIRTH

On Christmas Eve, my brothers and sisters and I—whoever was at home that particular year; there were thirteen of us in all—would gather around Mamma's chair, and she would read to us the story of Jesus' birth from the gospel of Luke. We knew every word, every character, every turn of the story; but still, it held our attention like little else could at that season of anticipation. I remember gazing at our nativity scene—its crude figures hand-carved from wood—and thinking that Christmas really was about a child, a baby, that Jesus had been a baby just like my brother Jimmy or sister Helen.

Today's Christmases seem more hectic, with less quiet time for families, but I make sure to gather my grandchildren on Christmas Eve and read to them the story of Jesus' birth, hoping that they will find, like I did so many years ago, a special connection to the child in the manger.

And it came to pass in those days, that there went out a decree from Caesar Augustus, that all the world should be taxed. . . . And all went to be taxed, ever one into his own city.—*Luke 2:1, 3*

And Joseph also went up from Galilee, out of the city of Nazare into Judaea, unto the city of David, which is called Bethlehen (because he was of the house and lineage of David:)—*Luke 2:4*

To be taxed with Mary his espoused wife, being great with child. And so it was, that, while they were there, the days were accomplished that she should be delivered.—*Luke 2:5, 6*

And she brought forth her firstborn son, and wrapped him in swaddling clothes, and laid him in a manger; because there was no room for them in the inn.—*Luke 2:7*

And there were in the same country shepherds abiding in the field, keeping watch over their flock by night.—*Luke 2:8*

And, lo, the angel of the Lord came upon them, and the glory of the Lord shone round about them: and they were sore afraid.—*Luke 2:9*

And the angel said unto them, Fear not: for, behold, I bring you good tidings of great joy, which shall be to all people.—*Luke 2:10*

For unto you is born this day in the city of David a Saviour, which is Christ the Lord.—*Luke 2:11*

And this shall be a sign unto you; Ye shall find the babe wrapped in swaddling clothes, lying in a manger.—*Luke 2:12*

And suddenly there was with the angel a multitude of the heavenly host praising God, and saying,—*Luke 2:13*

Glory to God in the highest, and on earth peace, good will toward men.—*Luke 2:14*

And it came to pass, as the angels were gone away from them into heaven, the shepherds said one to another, Let us now go even unto Bethlehem, and see this thing which is come to pass, which the Lord hath made known unto us.—*Luke 2:15*

And they came with haste, and found Mary, and Joseph, and the babe lying in a manger.—*Luke 2:16*

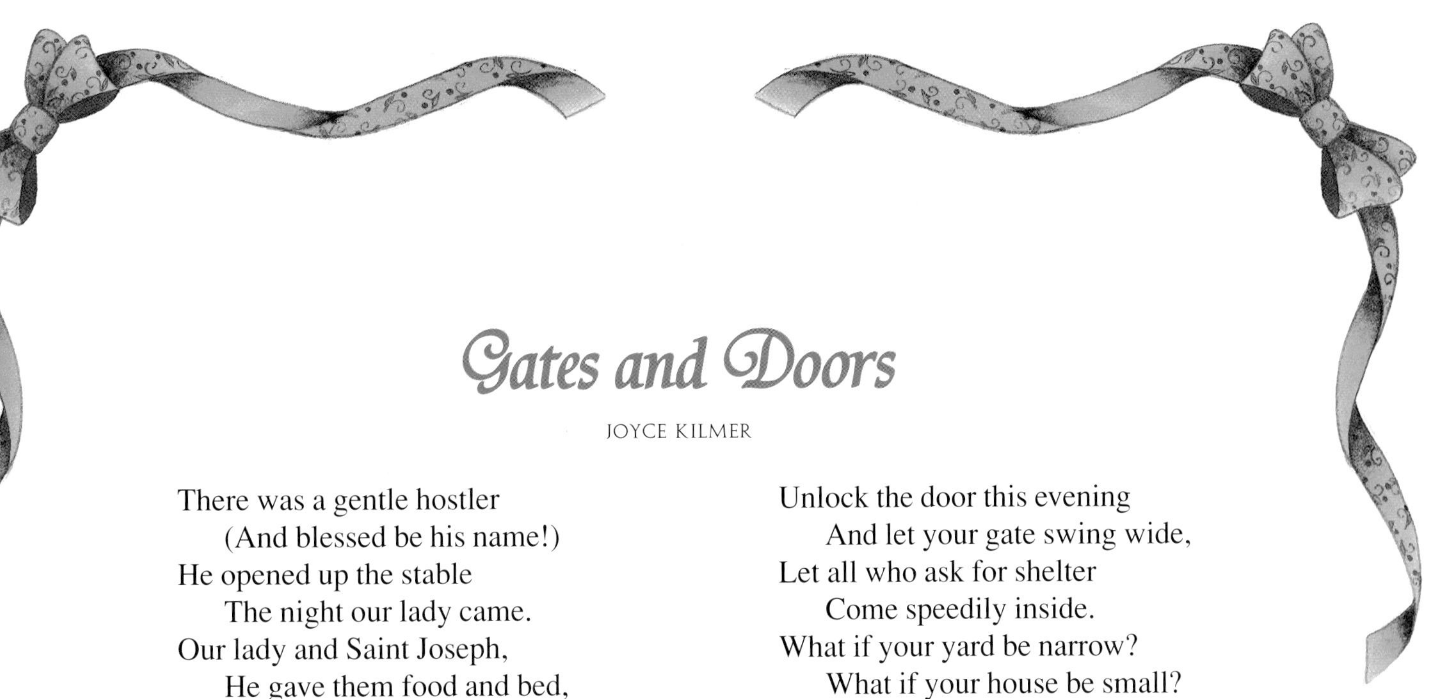

Gates and Doors

JOYCE KILMER

There was a gentle hostler
(And blessed be his name!)
He opened up the stable
The night our lady came.
Our lady and Saint Joseph,
He gave them food and bed,
And Jesus Christ has found him
A glory round his head.

So let the gate swing open
However poor the yard.
Lest weary people visit you
And find their passage barred;
Unlatch the door at midnight
And let your lantern's glow
Shine out to guide the traveler's feet
To you across the snow.

There was a courteous hostler
(He is in heaven tonight.)
He held our lady's bridle
And helped her to alight;
He spread clean straw before her
Whereon she might lie down,
And Jesus Christ has given him
An everlasting crown.

Unlock the door this evening
And let your gate swing wide,
Let all who ask for shelter
Come speedily inside.
What if your yard be narrow?
What if your house be small?
There is a guest is coming
Will glorify it all.

There was a joyous hostler
Who knelt on Christmas morn
Beside the radiant manger
Wherein his Lord was born.
His heart was full of laughter,
His soul was full of bliss
When Jesus, on His mother's lap,
Gave him His hand to kiss.

Unlock your heart this evening
And keep no stranger out,
Take from your soul's great portal
The barrier of doubt.
To humble folk and weary
Give hearty welcoming;
Your breast shall be tomorrow
The cradle of a King.

A Shepherd

HEYWOOD BROUN

The host of heaven and the angel of the Lord had filled the sky with radiance. Now the glory of God was gone and the shepherds and the sheep stood under dim starlight. The men were shaken by the wonders they had seen and heard and, like the animals, they huddled close.

"Let us now," said the eldest of the shepherds, "go even unto Bethlehem, and see this thing which has come to pass, which the Lord hath made known unto us."

The City of David lay beyond a far, high hill, upon the crest of which there danced a star. The men made haste to be away, but as they broke out of the circle there was one called Amos who remained. He dug his crook into the turf and clung to it.

"Come," cried the eldest of the shepherds, but Amos shook his head. They marveled, and one called out, "It is true. It was an angel. You heard the tidings. A Saviour is born!"

"I heard," said Amos. "I will abide."

The eldest walked back from the road to the little knoll on which Amos stood.

"You do not understand," the old man told him. "We have a sign from God. An angel commanded us. We go to worship the Saviour, who is even now born in Bethlehem. God has made His will manifest."

"It is not in my heart," replied Amos.

And now the eldest of the shepherds was angry.

"With your own eyes," he cried out, "you have seen the host of heaven in these dark hills. And you heard, for it was like the thunder when 'Glory to God in the highest' came ringing to us out of the night."

And again Amos said, "It is not in my heart."

Another shepherd then broke in. "Because the hills still stand and the sky has not fallen, it is not enough for Amos. He must have something louder than the voice of God."

Amos held more tightly to his crook and answered, "I have need of a whisper."

They laughed at him and said, "What should this voice say in your ear?"

He was silent and they pressed about him and shouted mockingly, "Tell us now. What says the God of Amos, the little shepherd of a hundred sheep?"

Meekness fell away from him. He took his hands from off the crook and raised them high.

"I too am a god," said Amos in a loud, strange voice, "and to my hundred sheep I am a saviour."

And when the din of the angry shepherds about him slackened, Amos pointed to his hundred.

"See my flock," he said. "See the fright of them. The fear of the bright angel and of the voices is still upon them. God is busy in Bethlehem. He has no time for a hundred sheep. They are my sheep. I will abide."

This the others did not take so much amiss, for they saw that there was a terror in all the flocks and they too knew the ways of sheep. And before the shepherds departed on the road to Bethlehem toward the bright star, each talked to Amos and told him what he should do for the care of the several flocks. And yet one or two turned back a moment to taunt Amos, before they reached the dip in the road which led to the City of David. It was said, "We shall see new glories at the throne of God, and you, Amos, you will see sheep."

Amos paid no heed, for he thought to himself "One shepherd the less will not matter at the throne of God." Nor did he have time to be troubled that he was not to see the Child who was come to save the world. There was much to be done among the flocks and Amos walked between the sheep and made under his tongue a clucking noise, which was a way he had, and to his hundred and to the others it was a sound more fine and friendly than the voice of the bright angel. Presently the animals ceased to tremble and they began to graze as the sun came up over the hill where the star had been.

"For sheep," said Amos to himself, "the angels shine too much. A shepherd is better."

With the morning the others came up the road from Bethlehem, and they told Amos of the manger and of the wise men who had mingled there with shepherds. And they described to him the gifts:

gold, frankincense, and myrrh. And when they were done they said, "And did you see wonders here in the fields with the sheep?"

Amos told them, "Now my hundred are one hundred and one," and he showed them a lamb which had been born just before the dawn.

"Was there for this a great voice out of heaven?" asked the eldest of the shepherds.

Amos shook his head and smiled, and there was upon his face that which seemed to the shepherds a wonder even in a night of wonders.

"To my heart," he said, "there came a whisper."

A Christmas Carol

EDGAR A. GUEST

God bless you all this Christmas Day
And drive the cares and grief away.
Oh, may the shining Bethlehem star
Which led the wise men from afar
Upon your heads, good sirs, still glow
To light the path that ye should go.

As God once blessed the stable grim
And made it radiant for Him;
As it was fit to shield His Son,
May thy roof be a holy one;
May all who come this house to share
Rest sweetly in His gracious care.

Within thy walls may peace abide,
The peace for which the Saviour died.
Though humble be the rafters here,
Above them may the stars shine clear,
And in this home thou lovest well
May excellence of spirit dwell.

God bless you all this Christmas Day;
May Bethlehem's star still light the way
And guide thee to the perfect peace
When every doubt and fear shall cease.
And may thy home such glory know
As did the stable long ago.

Arriving at the Christmas Party, New England
James R. Cooper/Superstock

Christmas Prayer

LORETTA BAUER BUCKLEY

On this hallowed eve of Christmas,
may you discover anew this splendor of the star,
the exultant song of herald angels,
the immeasurable love of Mary and Joseph.

May you find in the Child
of the manger all that you seek—
faith, hope, a deeper understanding
of charity and brotherly love.

In this golden hour of the miracle of Bethlehem,
may the beauty of quiet thoughts encompass your heart:
the tenderness of the mother's smile,
the adoration of humble shepherds.

With the brilliancy of the star,
may the year that lies ahead be lighted,
the days as a jeweled chain kept ever lustrous
with the divine love for which the Prince of Peace
was born into the world.

"Let Christmas be a bright and happy day; but let its brightness come from the radiance of the star of Bethlehem, and its happiness be found in Christ."

AUTHOR UNKNOWN

Grand Canyon, Arizona
Dick Dietrich Photography

INDEX